YORKSHIRE
CHURCHES

YORKSHIRE CHURCHES

Frank Bottomley

ALAN SUTTON

First published in the United Kingdom in 1993 by
Alan Sutton Publishing Limited
Phoenix Mill · Far Thrupp · Stroud · Gloucestershire

First published in the United States of America in 1993 by
Alan Sutton Publishing Inc
83 Washington Street · Dover · NH 03820

British Library Cataloguing in Publication Data

Bottomley, Frank
  Yorkshire Churches
  I. Title
  726.09428

  ISBN 0-7509-0344-9

Library of Congress Cataloging in Publication Data applied for

Jacket illustration: Humbleton, Humberside. *Derek G. Widdicombe (photo: Brian Jackson)*

Typeset in 11/14 Bembo.
Typesetting and origination by
Alan Sutton Publishing Limited.
Printed in Great Britain by
Redwood Books, Trowbridge.

CONTENTS

Introduction

The person visiting a church may have been impelled to do so by any of a number of motives. He may have come to pray or to sit in silence, to shelter from the rain or to satisfy his curiosity. He might be an amateur ecclesiologist, seeking out piscinas and aumbries, a brass-rubber or a student of costume and armour as portrayed in sepulchral monuments. He may be interested in stained glass or in armorials, or he may be seeking out examples of the art and craft which may be found in all churches: woodwork, needlework, or wrought iron, for instance. There may well be an element of nostalgia, or a vague curiosity about the past and the building's place in it.

Perhaps most often, he or she has just come to 'look round' and might well appreciate some guidance about what to look for and information about what may be found. It is chiefly for this last group that this book is written, although it is hoped that it will have something for every kind of church enthusiast and even encourage church-visiting among those who have, so far, not felt any inclination to do so.

Many parish churches are the oldest building in their town or village; some may be over 1,000 years old. (In spite of its omissions, 'Domesday Book' implies the existence in England of about 2,700 local churches in 1085.) In their long history these churches have changed, sometimes beyond recognition. Some bear the scars of war and a lot of the ancient ones show the marks of iconoclasm, vandalism and neglect. However, although their congregations have dwindled and almost everywhere the upkeep of the building is beyond the resources of those who generally use it, the vast majority do show much evidence of loving care and generous devotion.

The understanding of a parish church requires a minimal knowledge of their origin and purpose. Put simply, they were created to provide accommodation for communal worship by the Christians of a particular locality.

The first church was the 'upper room' where the disciples gathered to share the Last Supper with Christ. On that occasion, He added a new element to what was a Jewish ceremonial meal by taking bread and wine, blessing it, declaring that it was His body and blood and ordering His disciples to continue the rite as a memorial to Him. This they did and have continued to do, giving the service a variety of names: Liturgy, Eucharist, Mass.

In the early days, the rite maintained its original domestic setting in what were called 'house churches' – usually part of a large mansion owned by a wealthy member of the congregation. Even this undistinguished location had to be abandoned in times of persecution and, in Rome, the faithful sometimes sought shelter in the underground catacombs.

The situation changed in AD 313 when Constantine first declared that Christianity was a permitted religion within the Roman Empire and shortly afterwards it had imperial patronage. This led to the construction of purpose-built churches of the 'basilican' pattern which long provided the norm of church architecture. These basilicas were long rectangular buildings with the eastern end terminating in an apse, and with a nave which had aisles separated from the body of the church by a colonnade. The first churches in Roman Britain were of this type.

The Anglo-Saxon conquest provided a missionary situation in England which was met by monastic endeavour. This took two forms: the highly ascetic, but somewhat disorganized Celtic mission and the more moderate, organized Benedictine style. The latter was introduced from Rome by Augustine who reached England in AD 597. The pope who sent him (St Gregory) also planned the first diocesan organization of the country. The two missions were alike in faith but differed somewhat in practice, a situation which led to the Synod of Whitby in AD 664, which in turn resulted in an agreement that the whole country should adopt the Roman, Benedictine, form.

The mission largely operated from monastic centres called 'minsters' (from the Latin for a monastery) and these became the mother-churches of their district which often covered an extensive area. Parishes seem to have come into existence from two sources: the subdivision of the minster's area as its converts increased, and the foundation by nobles of churches to serve their estates. The first churches were built of timber but stone churches began to rise from an early date and Yorkshire possessed some by the seventh century. The outlines of the parochial system can be traced at least as far back as the time of Theodore (the Archbishop of Canterbury, who died in 690).

The status of 'parish church' was granted by the diocesan bishop who consecrated it and gave it its title when certain conditions had been fulfilled. Among these were an adequate endowment for the parish priest, absolute possession of the site and a building free from debt. Once the church was built, the rector was responsible for the chancel and the parishioners for the nave (and tower). In a large and scattered parish, supplementary churches might be provided for the convenience of those who lived far from the parish church. These were called 'chapels-of-ease' and might later acquire the status of parish church when a very large parish was subdivided.

By the 'title' of a church we mean its name, for example, Holy Trinity, St Mary, All Saints, etc. This is sometimes miscalled its dedication – a misleading usage as all churches are dedicated to Almighty God and the word 'church' or the northern 'kirk' is derived from a Greek word meaning 'house of the Lord'. Titles are interesting and may provide a variety of information or hints about missionary progress, the nature of the mission that established the church, fashions in devotion, and so forth. The most common title in Yorkshire is All Saints, closely followed by St Mary, with St Peter in third place. There are some very rare titles such as Ricarius (Aberford), Alkelda (Giggleswick and Middleham), Radegund (Scruton), Rumwald (Romualdkirk), while Eloy is unique in England. Yorkshire naturally celebrates its own saints: St Wilfrid of Ripon, St William of York, St Robert of Knaresborough, St Hilda of Whitby and St John of Beverley.

The Church in its Setting

As one approaches a church, it is worthwhile giving a little thought to its position. Is it on an elevated site? How does it relate to the town or village which it serves – is it central or peripheral and is there a reason for this? In a village, how is it related to the 'big house', or the castle of the town? (Cantley, for example, is out of the village but next to the hall, while Castle Bolton shelters under the castle walls.) When a church has no neighbours it is worthwhile asking what has happened to the settlement it was meant to serve. (At Harewood the village was moved to meet the lord's notions of aesthetics, at Lead it was destroyed in the battle of Towton.) Solitariness can be explained by population movement, and demography can solve many questions about changes in a church which continues to exist but is serving a larger or smaller congregation than that for which it was originally designed.

Even if a church was, and remained, of adequate size, its structure could be changed for a variety of reasons if the financial resources were available. The rector might want a more commodious chancel to enhance the dignity of worship; the laity might appreciate the advantages of adding a porch; greater bells might demand a substantial tower to accommodate them instead of the simple bell-cote which served for a single small bell. Above all, perhaps, was the constant desire to offer the best for God and the best would include the latest fashions in architecture, decoration and fitments. This desire for the best was not unmixed with more earthly motives of rivalry and the wish to outshine a neighbouring parish. Changes and developments in devotion could produce structural change in the provision of Lady chapels, chantries and accommodation for additional altars. Vestries/sacristies were something of a luxury and tend to be a later addition. There are medieval examples at, for example, Hackness, Gilling West, Roos, South Cowton.

Structural changes were naturally built in the best manner of their time and medieval architectural styles can provide a rough guide to the date of the whole or parts of a church building.

The earliest style is called Romanesque because its main feature, the 'round' (semicircular) arch, is derived from Roman building. In England it is subdivided into pre-Norman (Anglo-Saxon) and Norman (after 1066).

By the thirteenth century the round arch had been replaced by the 'pointed' arch – the hallmark of Gothic architecture. The change was slow and there is a period of Transition (about 1150–1200) when Norman and Gothic features are intermingled. The thirteenth-century style is usually called Early English and is marked by long narrow windows (lancets), often grouped together in twos, threes or fives with rudimentary tracery above. (Tracery is the ornamental stonework in a window head.)

Towards the end of the thirteenth century, the Decorated style emerged and lasted to about the middle of the fourteenth century. It is typified by the increasing elaboration of tracery and other decorative features (including the ogee arch, which utilizes a convex and concave shape on each side).

This was followed by the Perpendicular period which lasted almost two hundred years and is England's particular contribution to the international Gothic style. Perhaps its most characteristic feature (in spite of its name) is an increased horizontal emphasis.

There was little church-building after the Reformation until the great nineteenth-century explosion which mainly used neo-Gothic styles, but the rare intermediate examples are worth looking for. They include Fewston (largely rebuilt in 1697), the fine St John's in New Briggate, Leeds (1630s) and a number by the Yorkshire architect, John Carr (Horbury, for example, which dates from 1793).

Styles are most easily recognizable in windows, doorways and ornamental detail and the church explorer will greatly benefit from a modest ability to identify them. This can be fairly easily acquired by a little study of one of the many books on the subject, coupled with a visit to a church where the style of a particular period is dominant, for example, at Kirk Hammerton (Saxon), Adel and Birkin (Norman), Skelton (Early English), Bainton, Patrington (Decorated), and Beverley St Mary (Perpendicular).

When carrying out research, however, two points should be borne in mind. Firstly, dates of styles are very approximate. There is considerable overlap and, especially in country churches, stylistic features may be newly adopted in one place when they are already old-fashioned elsewhere. Secondly, doorways and windows, though comparatively easy to date roughly, are not a sure guide to the date of the masonry in which they are set, since they can both be inserted in older work or reused to make a feature in much later building.

The Churchyard

The possession of a cemetery or burial-ground was one of the characteristics of a parish church. Indeed, the grave-markers (hog-backs and crosses) which accompanied prestigious pre-Norman burials (there is a fine collection at Middleton) are often the only indications of the antiquity of a church site. Early ecclesiastical legislation required the defining of the churchyard in a substantial and permanent way by wall, ditch or bank, so the shape and extent may be interesting. A circular boundary, like the ones at Aldborough and Skipsea, is said to indicate a pre-Christian site consecrated to new use.

The modern boundary is usually a wall, often with the interior ground approaching its top due to changes in the level of the ground as a result of many burials. The structure of the wall may reward examination as it may contain reused ancient stones from the church. It might also have inserted tablets on which information is given. One such tablet at Scarborough indicates the whereabouts of Anne Brontë's grave, another at Hampsthwaite commemorates the gift of a stable, Emley has fragments from a house of the Knights Hospitaller which stood in the vicinity until the Dissolution. Nearby, and often built into the wall, mounting-steps for the benefit of the better-off who were not very athletic can frequently be found.

Devices to allow human, but not animal, access to the sacred ground can often display some ingenuity: kissing-gates, stiles of various design, and the interesting late seventeenth-century counterbalanced gate at Burnsall.

The traditional entrance is via a lych-gate, a covered access usually closed by a double gate. 'Lych' is derived from the Saxon word for a corpse and originally the roofed gate was provided with a table on which the body could be placed while the bearers rested to await the arrival of the priestly procession from the church. (There is a rare survival of the corpse-table at Wortley.) Medieval lych-gates were timber structures and therefore not likely to survive. Most existing lych-gates date from the present century or the end of the nineteenth. Although not especially old, nevertheless, they may well have their interest. The one at Hickleton is probably the reused church porch and inset in its wall is a *memento mori* of the medieval type – two skulls with the inscription 'Today for me, tomorrow for thee'. Snainton reuses a Norman arch, while Pickhill has a seventeenth-century Latin inscription from a parclose screen once in the church. At Sessay, the architect Butterfield (1848) combined the lych-gate with the boiler-house (disguised as a lodge) to provide a charming architectural feature and he has left a similar fine composition at Baldersby.

The churchyard itself has much to offer the interested explorer, perhaps the most obvious being the tombstones themselves. Few will date back further than the eighteenth century, although there is an interesting headstone from 1645 by the porch at Osbaldkirk. However, tombstones will provide examples of fine lettering (evident at Danby in Cleveland), varied symbolism (at Guisborough), and, not infrequently, significant information (for example, about longevity), and pathetic stories such as that of the drowned choirboys at Stillingfleet.

We may also find evidence of pandemic disease (Haworth), of the cost of the Industrial Revolution (Silkstone, Otley, Darfield, Kirkheaton), and of many a private tragedy in every cemetery. In contrast, there are curiosities like the carved organ at Kildwick or the Sevastapol trophy surmounting a family vault at Spennithorne and the memorial to an acrobat at Pocklington. Most graves, of course, have no memorial since only the comparatively affluent could afford enduring stone. Those that have gravestones include, among the better known, Anne Bronte (Scarborough), her sisters, Charlotte and Emily (Haworth), Sylvia Plath (Hebden Bridge), J.B. Priestley (Hubberholme), George Hudson, 'the railway king' (Scrayingham), Laurence Stern (Coxwold), Winifred Holtby, author of *South Riding* (Rudston), and 'Blind Jack of Knaresborough' (Spofforth). Dick Turpin lies in St George's churchyard at York.

There are multiple graves or 'family vaults' and occasionally pretentious mausolea, for example, at Kirkleatham and Little Ouseburn.

It was not the usual medieval practice to mark graves in the churchyard. The uncoffined bodies were only buried for a limited time as the space was constantly being reused and any bones found when digging a new grave were usually gathered into the charnel house (there is a rare survival of such at Beverley St Mary) which often stood at the edge of the cemetery.

There is a medieval slab with (illegible) black lettering at Otley and there are two famous table-tombs at Saxton and Loversall. The former belongs to Lord Dacre who was killed at the nearby battle of Towton (1461); the latter dates from the early fourteenth century but the occupant is unknown.

Skelbrook claims the grave of 'Little John', indicated only by two uninscribed markers. There is a rare marker from the mid-eleventh century at Mirfield.

The medieval churchyard ('God's Acre') was dedicated to its purpose in an elaborate ceremony but, even so, the part north of the church was regarded as less sanctified than that to the south and was rather reluctantly used as a burial-ground. The chief symbol of its hallowing was the universal churchyard cross which rose in solitary splendour above the hummocks of the surrounding graves. These crosses formed the termination of stone shafts which often rose from a stepped base. They were beautifully carved (often on both faces) with a representation of the crucifixion, the redeeming act which promised life after death. They were hated by the Reformers and consequently 'hewn down', sometimes level with the ground, leaving only a socket for the explorer to discover, or sometimes to a truncated shaft on which later might be erected a sundial (as at Long Preston) or garden ornament (South Anston). Some have been restored or replaced (Burghwallis, Hickleton) and a fine one was erected as a war memorial at Stainton. Occasionally, the original cross-head has been recovered and preserved (Garton, Sherburn-in-Elmet, Pocklington).

Fragments of these crosses are not without interest. There are remains of Norman churchyard crosses at Birstall, Hartshead, Rastrick, Rawmarsh. There is an unusually tall stump at Well; the remains of the base of a 'weeping cross' at Ripley and the remarkable object which has given its name to the village of Rudston (Rood stone). This, the tallest standing stone in Britain, originated as a monolith marking a prehistoric sacred site which was Christianized by carving its face with a rude cross. The cross is largely obliterated but the monolith still stands to a height of over 25 ft (7.8 m).

Cross stumps may have been used as whipping-posts and certainly were used for tying up dogs since the hooks for this purpose sometimes remain.

Some graveyards contain reminiscences of the 'Resurrection Men': criminals of the eighteenth and nineteenth centuries who stole bodies to sell to anatomy schools. Some tombs are surrounded by substantial grilles or iron fences to make exhumation more difficult. Pannal churchyard has a very heavy hollowed out stone, believed to be a 'mortsafe' which was placed over new graves for several weeks to foil body-snatchers. Bradfield has a rare survival in the 'Watch House' of 1745, built to accommodate the wardens who guarded the churchyard against human predators.

Various other objects may be discovered within the churchyard precincts. Parish stocks can be found at Burnsall, Marsden, Marske, and York St Saviours; ejected church furniture (a pillar piscina) at Adel; and fourteenth-century monuments at Kirby-in-Cleveland, Weaverthorpe and possibly Woolley. There may be fragments of broken, rejected or decayed masonry (pinnacles from the tower, for example) and stone coffins. These last come from within the church and were displaced when the floor was relaid, often as a result of the introduction of a heating system.

Medieval parsons, like many others, supplemented their diet by the fresh meat of pigeons or doves. At Elkstone, Glos., the underdrawing of the chancel comprises an enormous pigeon-cote with some 150 boxes. The usual location for the dove-cote was in the vicinity of the church and a rare eighteenth-century example survives at East Harsley. There are remains of another at Darrington: a square structure with a pyramid roof.

As the medieval churchyard was the only unencumbered space in the centre of the village, it was a location for religious processions and for the performance of religious plays. But it was also, in spite of regular admonitions from the church authorities, the scene of many secular activities: dances, markets, games (the 'buttress' in Eton Fives derives from its originating against a church wall) and archery practice. Archers often sharpened their arrows by rubbing them against the church's masonry, producing, as a result of continual use, the 'sharpening grooves' that can still be identified in many places.

The Exterior

Before entering the church it is worthwhile to have a good look at the exterior, both in general and in some detail. The usual obvious constituents are tower, nave, chancel and porch. If the church has a tower, does it (or the rest of the church) have battlements? Is there evidence that the tower is a later addition (not bonded into the main structure)? Is the tower in an unusual position (the commonest location is the west end of the church)? Does the tower possess any unusual features? At Royston, for example, there is a magnificent oriel window, at Hickleton and Whixley a saddle-back roof. There may be inscriptions, heraldry or other carving on the tower face (as at Barnborough and Goldsborough). Is there a spire or a spirelet? How are the upper floors reached and is there access to the stair turret from outside? Perhaps there is no tower but merely a bell-cote, as at Adel, which itself may be unusual, like the one found at Linton.

The body of the church consists of nave and chancel. Are they under one continuous roof, as often the case in Perpendicular churches (Skirlaugh), or are they structurally distinct? In the latter case, the chancel is usually lower than the nave and the latter's gable may contain a window (there is a rare example of this at Otley). Cases where the chancel is higher than the nave are unusual enough to be worth noting and (if possible) explaining (Low Catton, Harewood, Weston).

In Yorkshire, roofing material is usually stone flags, but there are exceptions such as the modern copper dome at Warmsworth. Is the roof line broken? This happens at Ryther, where there is a bell turret, and at Nether Poppleton and Stainburn, where there is a cote at the junction of the nave and chancel. Are there corbel-tables, gargoyles or other projections such as parapets or pinnacles?

A slow perambulation should indicate the number of entrances to the church. The main one is usually in the south wall of the nave near its western end. But there may be a western doorway, a northern one opposite the main entrance (sometimes fictionally called the 'devil's doorway') and often a priest's door in the south wall of the chancel.

Sometimes one or more of these doorways have been blocked up but traces of them may still be visible in the masonry (Barmston and Kirkby Overblow).

There may be other external signs of change: the insertion of larger windows or the blocked arches of a former aisle or chapel; walls butted together, rather than bonded; differences in the masonry (size and nature of building units, variations in thickness of mortar). Change in the pitch of a roof often leaves traces on an abutting wall (often the east face of the tower).

Sometimes there are unusual additions breaking the line of the wall such as the possible chantry at West Tanfield, or there may be embedded memorial tablets such as those at Weston.

Guidebooks may draw attention to the existence of a 'low side window'. This is a small opening, or extension of a larger window, whose sill is substantially lower than the level of the other windows. It tends to be inserted in the south wall of the chancel and its purpose is obscure. Perhaps it is best explained as a ventilation device to diminish the heat and fumes of the many candles that burnt in a medieval chancel or perhaps associated with a vanished cell for a recluse. Examples of low side windows can be found at Croft, Easby, Bardsey, Burnby, Lockington, Melsonby, North Otterington, Sancton, Scawton, Walton, Wilton, and elsewhere.

There are often sundials on the south side of the tower or nave. There is a famous Anglo-Saxon example at Kirkdale with others at Skelton (near Guisborough), Aldbrough, Edstone and Old Byland. The sundial at Weaverthorpe is Norman and records the (re)building of the church by Herbert Chamberlain. Many date from the eighteenth century or later (for example, those at Aberford, Croft, Kirkby Overblow, Long Preston, Marton, Sandal).

There is a miniature medieval version of a sundial, called a 'mass' or 'scratch' dial. It is usually found on or near the south porch and once informed parishioners of mass times. It is often difficult to see as it is not deeply marked. The 'mass dial' consists of a small circle (6 in or less in diameter) with a central depression and several radii in the lower half, sometimes with a small hole where they meet the circumference. There are examples at Armthorpe, Castle Bolton, Garton-on-the-Wolds, Goldsborough and elsewhere. The sundial was eventually displaced by the turret clock which was invented in the Middle Ages as an 'alarm clock' to waken the monks for the early morning offices. It might have existed in wealthy parish churches but, if so, it did not survive the Reformation. Most existing church clocks date from the nineteenth century, but they are worth more than a casual glance. Some are inscribed with a suitable motto and they often have a pleasant face and well-designed hands (for example, the early nineteenth-century clock at Leathley, York St Denys and the fine clock at St Martin-le-Grand which is supported over the pavement by an attractive bracket). At Whitgift, the figure 13 replaces the normal 12, while at Ravenfield the clock has only a single hand. The clock at Kildwick has a square face. There is rather an unattractive electric clock in the west gable at Oswaldwick.

The study of clock faces may well lead to questions being raised. Why, for example, is the normal IIII on a clock-face replaced by IV (economy of space or material?), and why are some clock faces blue, like those at Addingham, Catterick, Hampsthwaite, Panall and Thirsk, among others. (A common explanation is that blue is the traditional colour of the Blessed Virgin Mary, but this is unsatisfactory.)

The western face of the tower often has a niche which once bore a statue of the church's patron saint. The splendid fifteenth-century tower at Tickhill retains its original statuary (as does Beeford), though the pair of niches at Barwick-in-Elmet are empty. External niches occur elsewhere, in the gable of the porch or in recesses of Perpendicular buttresses, for example. North Frodingham has a very pretty Perpendicular niche on the south wall of the nave with a restored statue. The splendid Transitional west front at Nun Monkton has a set of fine niches but the surviving statuary is much decayed.

Small external sculpture is worth looking for. It occurs frequently in the terminations of drip-moulding over windows or the arch of the porch. Norman churches may possess elaborately carved corbel-tables as at Adel, while North Newbald has a fine majestas over one of its doorways. The medieval carver found scope to exercise his imaginative and manual skills in the decoration of gargoyles (waterspouts) and grotesques (non-functional). Examples at Barnby Dun, Bainton, and so on, are worth examining, preferably with field-glasses, as are the gable crosses which display many inventive variations on the simple theme of a cross.

As far as the general structure of the church is concerned, some note should be taken of the material. It is usually stone, but it may be brick or clay. Stone comes in many forms: pebble, rubble or ashlar (cut stone). If it is the latter, it may be worth examining whether it is laid in courses and, if so, whether the mortar joints are thick or thin. The former tends to indicate early Norman work as does the practice of laying them in diagonal courses (herring-bone work).

Additional interest might be gained from the ability to recognize the type of stone used – Tadcaster limestone and Pennine gritstone are two. In this respect, A. Clifton Taylor's *The Pattern of English Building* is strongly recommended.

REGIONAL STYLES

After looking at a number of exteriors, the explorer might ask himself whether there is such a thing as a typically Yorkshire church. He could well answer in the negative but be aware that there are churches which do seem characteristic of particular parts of the county, for example, the long, low silhouette of a Dales' church which is also often found in the West Riding. There are also what might be taken as local idiosyncrasies in the design of particular features, the provision of niches in the piers of a nave arcade, for instance, found at Broughton, Kirkby Malham and Bracewell – all in the West Riding – or the capping of a tower with a truncated 'spike' rather than a spire which occurs at Knaresborough and Barnbrough. A low, widespread, sturdy tower with an embattled parapet is also said to be a characteristic of West Riding churches. More clearly 'local' are the corbelled-out parapets which occur on many churches around Leeds (Bardsey, Thorner, Guiseley and Elland, which is said to be machicolated) and Batley which has a very military appearance. The fashion seems to have spread to the North Riding (Bainton) and continued in the tower at Arkendale (dating from 1873).

Another Yorkshire pattern has been discerned in the 'fretted fringe-like patterns' of some tower parapets which results from setting much-crocketted pointed arches between the battlements of some Perpendicular towers. This feature is visible at Beeford, Holme-on-Spalding Moor, Hull Holy Trinity, Thirsk and Tickhill.

In the East Riding there appears to have been a fashion of decorating towers with eight pinnacles instead of the usual four (Kirk Ella, Preston), while the North Riding seems to have produced a local type of tower stair-turret, exemplified at Kirklington. The parish churches of the North Riding tend to be low and long, often without battlements or even parapets. The enamelled tiles on the roofs at Drax, Fishlake and Snaith can leave a rather 'Dutch' impression on visitors to the Selby area. Some have identified a 'Malton group' of spires (for example, at Malton, Rillington, Wintringham) and a regional Perpendicular style in Craven (Burnsall, Kirkby Malham, Sedbergh, Skipton (which incorporates some Decorated work) and Thornton-in-Craven).

To revert to an earlier period, the Norman ornament called 'beakhead' is more frequent in Yorkshire than anywhere else in England and therefore might be described as a local characteristic.

Almost inevitably, visitors have found that the gaunt churches in the moorland valleys around Haworth carry with them something of a common air of 'Wuthering Heights'.

PORCHES

Anglo-Saxon churches possessed porches or porticoes but there is little evidence of this amenity being generally provided for Norman churches, although there are examples at Shiptonthorpe and Wadworth. It is possible that there were simple wooden structures which have vanished without trace, but it is difficult to believe that such an elaborate portal as that at Adel was ever enclosed within a porch of any kind. The same would be true of Garton-on-the-Wolds.

Yet, during the Gothic period, porches eventually became *de rigueur* to provide the setting for a number of church services and ceremonies, of which the most important was marriage. (We remember that Chaucer's 'Wife of Bath' had married 'five husbands, all at the church door'.)

Originally, many of these porches must have been timber and have rarely survived in Yorkshire (Thorpe Salvin is exceptional). There is a post-medieval timber porch at Little Ouseburn and another at Foston (dating from 1911).

Where money or suitable stone was lacking, a porch might be constructed of brick. The seventeenth-century porches at Harpham and Welwick are examples of this, and the early nineteenth-century porch at Bossall is floored with brick.

As a stone-built porch is something of a luxury, parishes often had to wait for some wealthy benefactor to provide it. (The fine porch at South Cowton has an upper chamber carried on a tunnel-vault and bears an inscribed request that the parishioners, in return for his generosity, should pray for the good estate of Sir Richard Conyers.) Consequently, porches might be added to a church at any period – at Wath the porch was added in *c*. 1300, at Whixley in 1300–10, an outstanding example was added at Beverley St Mary in 1420, at Weston in 1686, the porch at Otley is Georgian and at Skipton it is dated 1850.

The Perpendicular period was a time of much church-building, rebuilding and modification, and many porches were built in the fifteenth and early sixteenth centuries. These include Bowes, which was built in accordance with a will of 1404, Worsborough, with its fine ceiling and door, and Marske, which has a monumental sixteenth-century inscription of unknown reference. Whenby has a good Perpendicular porch with two windows on either side. Kirby Hill (Ravensworth) is battlemented and attached to the contemporary south aisle. The little porch at Kellington is not only battlemented but furnished with gargoyles. South Kirkby has an elaborate south porch of two storeys and a simpler one facing north. Thorne is even more decorative, with an oriel window in its upper storey. Scarborough, like South Cowton, has an upper storey raised on a tunnel-vault. Easby, of the same period, has a similarly supported upper storey (originally two) and unique large aumbries. It is suggested that these were used to store the alms in kind which were distributed to the poor when the church was in the hands of the Premonstratensian monks.

Perhaps at this point we might ask what the upper floor of a porch was used for. It is not always certain, as there are several possibilities. It could have provided occasional or emergency accommodation for a visiting priest or chantry chaplain but this is unlikely as few, if any, porch chambers show any signs of the facilities necessary for residence. In some cases, it provided security for valuable possessions such as archives, infrequently used plate, or relics (as was the case at Selby – though this was a monastic church). If, in the north wall, there was a window giving on to the church interior, it could be a 'watching chamber' from which an eye could be kept on special treasures within the church. But such windows are extremely rare. Most likely, it was a place of business used for such activities as the signing of contracts and agreements, and meetings between the rector and church officials. It was occasionally used as a schoolroom and often for storage. In post-reformation times it could house almost anything from the parish library to the arms of the local militia.

There is sometimes a statue niche in the exterior face of the gable of the porch (for example, at Campsall). It is now usually empty but Shiptonthorpe retains a twelfth-century statue of a bishop and Kirby Hill (Ravensworth) has a small grotesque statue which may represent King David.

Stone benches were often provided along the walls (as at Croft). Sometimes these are of a later date than the porch itself and may make use of cannibalized material. This economy is frequently visible in the walls which often display reused carved fragments, particularly broken coffin covers (Conisborough, Hampsthwaite, Kirby Hill).

Medieval churches always provided a stoup for holy water near the entrance and, unless it was just inside the church door, it was located in the right-hand inner corner of the porch. There is an interesting example in the thirteenth-century church at Gate Helmsley where the stoup is made from a scalloped Norman capital. At Patrick Brompton the base of a round pier has been recycled to provide the stoup. Stoups tended to be smashed or torn out at the Reformation and occasionally may survive in the churchyard, as at Stainburn and, possibly, Adel. Before leaving the porch it is worth looking for small-scale sculpture, particularly round the doorway into the church. There are some unusual examples at Eastrington, Newton Kyme, Barnbrough, Bowes and Ricall.

DOORS AND DOORWAYS

The main entrance to a church (almost always on the south) received considerable elaboration, possibly because of the symbolism of Christ's statement, 'I am the Door'. Norman doorways are particularly rich and often were reset when the church was enlarged by adding a south aisle. They even survived nineteenth-century rebuilding at Thorp

Arch and Thorpe Bassett and fine fragments of a late Norman doorway are preserved inside the nineteenth-century Boroughbridge.

Yorkshire possesses many excellent Norman doorways and a selection should include Adel, Alne, Barton-le-Street, Brayton, Fishlake, Foston, North Newbald, Riccall, Stillingfleet, Thorpe Salvin, Wighill. Though the carving ('weighing of a soul') is crude, Danby Wiske might be mentioned because it has the only Norman tympanum *in situ*.

There are good Early English doorways at Skelton (near York), Filey and Hemingborough, Decorated doorways at Campsall, Patrington, and Perpendicular ones at Beverley St Mary and Thirsk.

A small doorway in the south wall of the chancel is the 'priest's door'. It antedates the provision of vestries and was provided so that the priest could gain direct access to the sanctuary where his vestments would have been laid out ready on the high altar. There is a Norman example at Farnham, and ogee-headed examples at Panall and Barmston.

Sometimes there is a north doorway (now often blocked) opposite the main (south) entrance. Its purpose was to allow a returning procession to re-enter the church. It tends to exist only in small churches which had no space for an internal ambulatory. Where there is a major doorway on the north side, it is a probable indication that the township which the church served had developed in that direction and therefore this more convenient access had been provided.

A church may possess a western entrance of some magnificence, such as those at Campsall, Bolton Abbey and Nun Monkton. This entrance was not generally used but retained for major occasions such as the entry of the Palm Sunday procession, the formal visitation of a bishop and perhaps the attendance of some great secular lord such as the king.

From the doorway we turn to the door itself. This was always a serviceable and substantial oak construction, often composed of more than one layer and further strengthened with studs and other ironwork. Unusually large doors had an inset smaller door or wicket, sometimes called a 'Judas door'. Ottringham has an ogee-headed wicket dating from the fourteenth century or earlier.

Medieval doors and/or their metal fittings sometimes survive. There are attractive bronze knocker-rings from the Norman period at Adel and York All Saints Pavement and there are a number of hinges from the same period. The remarkable ironwork on the south door at Stillingfleet might be even older than the Norman doorway in which it is set, for it has pronounced Viking characteristics. The simpler work on the north door is probably Norman. The 'wild and abundant ironwork' on the west door at Leathley probably dates from the twelfth century and the more restrained work at Hickleton and Kirby Hill is likely to be of the same vintage.

There are thirteenth-century hinges at Burghwallis, Hooton Pagnell and Willerby and those at Seamer are as old or even older. About this time the medieval blacksmiths developed the fashion of opening out the ends of the hinges into a great C which some have seen as a reference to St Clement, the patron saint of the blacksmiths. Examples of this can be found at Hooton Pagnell, and some date these as early as *c.* 1100.

The design of doors reached its climax in the Perpendicular period when wealthy churches acquired elaborately carved and traceried constructions. Though they have lost their colourful paintwork and the woodwork is much worn or defaced, something of their original splendour can be imagined from surviving examples. The handsome south door at Worsborough, *c.* 1480, has tracery and an inscription commemorating its two donors.

There are traceried doors at Brompton, Barton-in-the-Forest, Healaugh, Middleton, and at York St Cuthbert Peaseholme Green and Holy Trinity Micklegate – all probably dating from the fifteenth century. Thirsk has two doors dating from the early fifteenth century, a traceried south one and a simpler north.

Later work worthy of special mention might include the studding at Bilton Ainstey (dated 1633), the north door of 1694 at Winestead, the seventeenth-century door at Kirkby Wharfe with its 'broad vertical bands of twined scrolly strands', and the eighteenth-century west door at Beverley Minster.

The Interior

Having passed through the doorway, proceed to the back of the church, stand in the centre and take in a general impression. Is it of light and space, gloom and clutter, colour, dignity, calm and reverence or what? There used even to be a characteristic country church smell, compounded of dust, damp and paraffin. The last has now gone and might be replaced by a faint trace of incense.

You will be standing with your back to the west wall and probably the tower. In front is the nave, possibly with aisles and/or side chapels. A larger church might receive extra light from an upper row of windows (clerestory). Have a look at the roof, it may well repay study.

Beyond the body of the nave (a word derived from the Latin for 'ship' since it is a symbol of the 'ark of salvation') lies the chancel, usually defined by an arch and possibly a screen ('chancel' comes from a word meaning 'openwork screen'). The chancel normally has two divisions: the quire with stalls for the ministers and singers and, beyond, the sanctuary or altar area, usually marked off by low rails.

This part of the church is usually very well lit – not only by the windows in the walls of the chancel but by a great east window over the altar. Warmsworth and Hilton are probably the only churches in the county which lack an east window. The situation at Bolton Abbey is different again as the present east wall was erected when the priory was dissolved to preserve the parochial nave from the ruination which befell the rest of the church.

The nave–chancel arrangement is sometimes called a 'two-cell plan' with a tower sometimes adding a third. This is the simplest plan but may be complicated by the development of aisles, possibly extended to the chancel, or by the addition of one or more chapels. A favourite plan, when resources allowed, was the symbolic cruciform layout with the nave in the long arm, transepts crossing, and the chancel in the eastern arm with a tower where the four arms met (an arrangement seen at Cottingham and Filey). The part of the church where the main altar is, or was, situated is always called the east end, irrespective of its actual compass direction. The other parts of the church, the north aisle, south porch, west tower, are named by their relation to this primal position.

If the exigencies of the site allowed, medieval churches were planned so that their major axes lay east–west. There were doubtless symbolic reasons for this: light was a very acceptable symbol of the divine, Christ was the Sun of Righteousness, the Day-Spring from on high, and so on. Variations in orientation have been explained as the consequence of seasonal differences in the point of sunrise.

Though there was a strong symbolic element in the planning and ornament of medieval churches, some alleged symbolism is 'post facto', e.g. explaining a badly laid-out chancel in a cruciform church ('weeping chancel') as symbolizing Christ's head bent on the cross.

Having literally orientated ourselves and perhaps acquired a guidebook, we proceed to a more detailed examination of the contents of the nave, beginning with the font.

THE FONT

Traditionally, the font is placed near the door to symbolize the fact that entry into the church is through baptism. Usually it is free-standing but occasionally it may be enclosed in a baptismal chapel (baptistery), sometimes situated within the tower. The font is the most important item of nave furniture and was treated with the utmost reverence because of its association with the first, and most necessary sacrament. Consequently, it was usually retained even when the entire church was rebuilt and thus is often the oldest object in the church. The nineteenth-century churches of Rushton Parva and Snainton have Norman fonts.

No definitely Anglo-Saxon fonts are known in the county but there are well over sixty survivals of every kind from the Norman period. They are monolithic and usually tub- or drum-shaped, although there are some square ones, at Marske, for example. The decoration may be simple (often cable pattern, zigzag or arcades) or the font may be covered by complex iconography. Of the former, there are examples at Easby, Grinton and Newton-in-Cleveland in the North Riding, at Carnaby, Rudston, Weaverthorpe (the East Riding), and Linton, Stainburn and Rotherham (the West Riding). More complex examples may be found at West Rounton (the North Riding), Langtoft and North Grimston (the East Riding), and Cowlam, Ingleton and Thorpe Salvin (the West Riding).

Thirteenth-century fonts are rarer, but may be found at Low Catton, Hornsea (Purbeck marble), Norton, near Doncaster, Thornton Steward, Settrington, Gilling West and North Newbold. The font at Tunstall has an interesting history. It was manufactured in c. 1300 but about a century later the bowl was replaced. Later still, possibly in the nineteenth century, the composite creation was entirely recut.

Bridlington has an early fourteenth-century Decorated font in black Frosterley marble. Hedon, Hull Holy Trinity and Keyingham have somewhat earlier examples of the same style, while the font at Patrington perhaps dates from a little later.

There are Perpendicular fonts in black Frosterley marble at

Startforth, South Kilvington, Catterick, and Richmond – the last has an inscription indicating that its donor was Lord Scrope. Frequently the benefactor was commemorated by the heraldic shields which are a common decoration on the bowls of Perpendicular fonts. Other examples can be found at Sancton, Yarm, Beverley St Mary, Conisborough, Cowthorpe, Darfield, Fishlake, and Tickhill.

One of the most interesting fonts in the county is that at Goodmanham, a highly decorated Perpendicular piece with an inscription stating the necessity of baptism and recording the names of its donors, one of whom was the parish priest. It is dated *c.* 1530.

FONT COVERS

The medieval honouring of the font was not confined to the costly carving (originally coloured and gilded) but extended to its adornment with a cover of rich material called a 'font cloth'. It was also secured with a lockable lid to prevent abuse of the consecrated baptismal water. (Remains of the staple and hinge to secure this lid may be found, but more frequently, there only remains the signs of damage done to the bowl when the Reformers tore them out.) Not content with a merely utilitarian lid, medieval devotion often transformed the font cover into an elaborate spire-like structure of carved, coloured and gilded wood.

Earlier efforts seem to have been largely replaced during the Perpendicular period, so surviving medieval font covers date from the late Middle Ages. One of the best Yorkshire examples is at Almondbury, but there is a glorious example at Halifax, while Hackness possesses a fine three-tier cover which was probably made in the early sixteenth century. Selby, though it was a monastic church, was so much used by the townsfolk that the monks provided the nave with a font and a cover that survived the fire of 1912. The font cover at Grinton is said to date from the fifteenth century, and the much restored example at Thirsk dates from the same period as does the 10 ft high font cover at Middleham.

Bradford, made a cathedral in 1919, retains a font cover from the time when it was a medieval parish church. This is similar to that at Halifax: a 'spectacular Late Gothic piece, tall, with tall spire, and a filigree of buttresses and tracery' (Pevsner).

The few survivals largely come from wealthy medieval towns but the oldest (dated 1352) may be found in the small village church of Well. As the niches in the canopies often contained statuettes and the whole was often crowned with some symbolic image, reforming vandals had a religious excuse for their destruction.

DESTRUCTION AND REPLACEMENT

The iconoclasm which wrecked font covers sometimes extended to the smashing of the fonts themselves by the Puritan reformers. They seem to have been particularly zealous in the West Riding area where many churches had their fonts destroyed. When Charles II was restored to the throne in 1660 the ruined fonts were replaced by new ones of a utilitarian (and cheaper) design. The font bowls are inscribed with the date of their replacement and often with the initials of the churchwardens responsible. Darrington has an inscription recording the necessary refurbishment after the disaster of the Commonwealth. Kirby Sigston has a typical font inscribed with the date 1662 and initials. Other fonts with the same date include Northallerton, Rothwell, Wensley (all with contemporary covers), Sandal, Batley, Ecclesfield and Burneston. Some churchwardens must have acted extremely quickly for Keighley's font is dated 1661, as is Wakefield's. Other churchwardens seem to have been a little slower off the mark. Fonts at East Ardsley, Kippax, Birkin, Kellington, Yafforth and Marske (which has slightly more decoration than the usual 'utility' version) all bear the date 1663. So does the cup-shaped font, with big irregular flutings on the bowl, at Emley, which dates from the later seventeenth century. The fonts at York St Olave (an octagonal goblet) and Pickhill are dated 1673 and 1686 respectively. Walkington seems to have had something of a general refurbishment in the seventeenth century when the churchwardens not only provided a new pulpit but a square font with moulded base and moulded top. The presence of an Elizabethan font at Marr and the more elaborate one at Huddersfield, dated 1570 and bearing the contemporary Royal Arms, may be an indication of earlier damage than that caused in the 1600s. The font at Edlington is possibly dated 1590 and may be there due to similar circumstances.

There are a number of eighteenth-century fonts: that at Kirkleatham is contemporary with the church. It is a restrained piece consisting of a bowl and baluster of white and dark green marble.

Pevsner describes the large fluted urn which does duty as a font at Croft as 'unusual and effective'. There is a font dated 1718 at Kirkthorpe, a primitive stone baluster of the eighteenth century at Hilton, and an elaborate work at Denton (1776) by the Yorkshire architect Carr. There are other examples at Langthwaite, Levisham and a nice example, characteristic of its period (1777), at Rokeby. The eighteenth-century baluster and bowl at Allerton Mauleverer would make a beautiful bird-bath. Hornby has a font, given in 1783, which is a well-carved and very good imitation of a Decorated piece. The font at Seamer, near Stokesley, is said to have been presented in 1798, having allegedly been brought from the ruins of a church in Alexandria. Pevsner describes it as 'a very coarse baluster or over-moulded pillar'. In contrast, York Holy Trinity has a good font (1717) with a magnificent contemporary cover and there is another eighteenth-century example at Holy Trinity Micklegate, also with a contemporary cover. Bridlington Christchurch (1841) has an eighteenth-century font and cover from York Minster. Swine has an example of the eighteenth-century 'Gothick' manner.

Apart from those in contemporary churches, there are nineteenth-century fonts elsewhere. Old Malton has one imitating the medieval example at Hull Holy Trinity. In the vestry at Hawes is another, made of black marble with a square baluster stem which supports a white earthenware bowl (inscribed 1822). There is an ornate High Victorian specimen at Manfield and the nineteenth-century church at Escrick is worth mentioning because of its contemporary font. This is a delicate affair of white marble where the bowl is supported by back to back male and female cherubs and the font is placed in a semi-hexagonal baptistery whose vault is supported by red Devonshire marble columns.

Some twentieth-century examples might be offered. The seventeenth-century church at East Harsley, much modified in the nineteenth century, has a modern font consisting of a massive tapered stone beaker with a shallow copper bowl set in its upper surface. At Bishop Wilton, in 1902, Temple Moore created a fine 'medieval' piece. Besides its medieval font, Whixley has a modern version – a tapering wooden hexagon with a shallow copper bowl let into its top.

The attempt to make good some of the damage caused by over-zealous Reformers was not confined to fonts. It extended also to their covers. There are Elizabethan examples at Slaidburn and a similar one at Mitton (1593). At Methley, a local painter, Richard Webster, left a bequest (in 1584) for the replacement of the font cover in his parish church. It is a substantial piece, though perhaps a bit rustic: octagonal with two tiers of openwork with a spire over. The rather elementary design at Edlington probably dates from *c.* 1590.

There are a number of Jacobean examples of varying sophistication and complexity. Calverley has a very good piece with two tiers of tracery and foliage, surmounted by a spire. Skipton has a more advanced version of the Methley piece and Bolton Percy has another handsome seventeenth-century font cover. The cover at Eastrington dates from the same century and has a curious crane to lift it. Royston and North Newbold both have font covers dating from the seventeenth century and Harthill has an unusual Jacobean example. The Perpendicular font at Richmond was provided with a replacement cover in the early seventeenth century. Leake has an uncommonly substantial piece also from the seventeenth century, heavily moulded and topped by an acorn. The Jacobean cover at Yarm was topped with a knob in the eighteenth century. The cover at Stanwick is also Jacobean, as is the somewhat awkward design at Husthwaite. This last might be compared with the elegant simplicity of the example at Raskelf. Stanwick, Ilkley, Darfield and Fishlake have Jacobean font covers (the last somewhat rustic). Northallerton has a straightforward piece of 1662 and that at Scawton is of about the same period, an octagonal 'top hat' with handle, described by Pevsner as 'effective'. Rillington also has a seventeenth-century font cover.

Styles were slow to develop in country districts and many supposedly 'Jacobean' pieces were actually made in 1662 or later (the fine examples at Arksey and Rothwell, for instance). The 'Jacobean' font cover at Long Preston is actually dated 1726! There is a big, rather heavy example at Darfield, and that at Fewston might be described as 'Jacobean', though it almost certainly belongs to the restoration of 1697. The same description might apply to the substantial work at Knaresborough, with supporting bracket and crane (from *c.* 1700).

There is more characteristic eighteenth-century work in York at Holy Trinity Goodramgate and Holy Trinity Micklegate (the latter is dated 1717, as is the font cover at St Martin-le-Grand). The example at Wintringham (1736) is painted with cherubs in brown and black. There are simpler eighteenth-century designs at Nunnington, Bossall, Brodsworth and a massive nineteenth-century one at Kildwick.

A number of font covers were made in the present century.

Boynton has an unusual design by Francis Johnson, Helmsley a tall piece by G.G. Pace and, somewhat earlier (1902), Temple Moore produced a characteristic work for Bishop Wilton. In 1921, Eric Gill designed an octagonal font cover for Adel. Its decoration follows the medieval tradition of the 'seven sacrament font' (common in East Anglia) but the Anglican authorities asked for the omission of the sacrament of penance. There is an impressive twentieth-century font cover with contemporary chandeliers at Bradfield.

PAUSE FOR REFLECTION

The neighbourhood of the font is a good place to pause. Nearby is usually a book table which may offer picture postcards and useful guides. The table itself may be an antique, even a rejected communion table. In the vicinity may be a list of former incumbents, often with a tale to tell to the observer. There may also be a set of bread shelves or a cupboard from which a dole was once given to the parochial poor (there is a Jacobean example at Scawton; an example dating from c. 1700 at York St Martin-cum-Gregory; and a handsome eighteenth-century piece with pedimented top at Aldborough). In the eighteenth century the existence of this and other parochial charities had to be displayed, resulting in the creation of Charity Boards which may also be visible. These list the charities and give their nature and, though obsolete, may survive, as they do at Middleham, South Cave, and York St Martin-cum-Gregory. At Wold Newton, they are grouped at the west end of the church along with the Commandment Boards and the Royal Arms (1829).

The Royal Arms, which identified patriotism with membership of the established Church, originally tended to be erected in the place of the rood in the chancel arch (they are incorporated in the post-Reformation screen at Bempton). In modern times, they have been removed to a less obtrusive position (at Grinton they are in the vestry). The interested explorer might try to collect a 'set' of Royal Arms from Elizabeth I to Elizabeth II. Halifax and Slaidburn both have two examples but generally the earlier one was replaced or repainted. Hedon has an Elizabeth I (1585), the earlier seventeenth-century examples probably perished during the Commonwealth but Burstwick has a rare Restoration example with the arms of Charles II and a contemporary painting of his father's execution on the back.

Others exist at Hackness and Silkstone (William and Mary), Ingleby Arncliffe (William III), Bossall (Anne), Giggleswick, Kildwick and Swillington (George I), Stillington (George II), Wensley and York St Michael-le-Belfrey (George III). There is another Hanoverian at Coxwold and several Victorias, at Nether Poppleton, Sewerby and Wold Newton, for example. I know of no twentieth-century examples except that of George VI at Ingleby Arncliffe.

Elizabeth I ordered the introduction of the Commandment Boards as an edifying feature of her new church settlement. They were usually fixed on the east wall of the church on either side of the communion table to display the Ten Commandments. They were sometimes supplemented by a board on which were written the Lord's Prayer and the Apostles' Creed.

Up to the middle of the nineteenth century these boards were standard and universal furniture in Anglican parish churches but now rarely survive (but they remain at Bedale). The Commandment Boards were often flanked by painted figures of Moses and Aaron, of which there is a unique Yorkshire example at Allerton Mauleverer. These figures also exist in painted glass at Myton-on-Swale and Yarm has a Peckitt window showing Moses delivering the Law (1768). The west window at Barton (1841) has no figure work at all, just the inscription of the Commandments, Creed and Lord's Prayer in the manner of Commandment Boards.

STAINED GLASS

In spite of its cost, the use of coloured glass seems as old as church-building. Anglo-Saxon fragments have been found in association with the remains of churches of this period, but it was not until the twelfth century that its symbolic and edifying parallels were realized and exploited.

Abbot Suger, of St Denys near Paris, saw light as the best symbol of God and is said to have initiated Gothic architecture through his desire to increase the size of windows. This development continued throughout the Gothic period so that, by its end, Perpendicular churches could be described as 'more glass than wall'.

Unfortunately, glass is a fragile material. The lead in which it is set needs frequent renewal, otherwise it perishes and leaves the glass subject to the violence of winds and storm. It is, however, even more subject to the violence of man, particularly of those who saw 'graven images' as an offence to God. Much was deliberately destroyed at the Reformation and even more in the storm of iconoclasm associated with the Commonwealth. The medieval glass of York was saved through the specific terms of the surrender of the city to General Fairfax.

Consequently entire medieval windows survive at York, not only in the Minster (where, among much else, there is a twelfth-century panel, claimed to be oldest in country), but also in many parish churches, of which All Saints North Street is the most outstanding. Elsewhere, the remains are fragmentary and generally confined to the small tracery of a window head, out of the reach of a pike and not easy to hit with a stone. Occasionally there are more substantial remains, as at Selby where there is a (much restored) great window of c. 1340. Smaller windows, more or less complete, may be found at Bolton Percy, Methley, Wintringham and Wycliffe.

Even these smaller relics may have particular interest. The east window at Ingleby Arncliffe, for example, preserves fourteenth-century fragments said to be from Mount Grace; the windows at Middleham include a representation of the martyrdom of St Alkelda. The destroyed stained glass was replaced by plain but occasionally a decorative effect was supplied by the arrangement of leading (as at Halifax).

Coloured glass returned at various times as heraldic decoration – at Goldsborough (1696), High Melton (eighteenth century), and at Kildwick and Wentworth. Figures in the form of medallion heads occur in eighteenth-century glass at Conisborough and religious subjects make a tentative appearance in eighteenth-century fragments at Allerton Mauleverer. The east window of the eighteenth-century church at Denton has both elaborate heraldry and a religious centre-piece. The names of glass-painters are made known at some churches – Henry Gyles (c. 1640–1709) at Farnley, William Peckitt (1731–95) at Harpham.

It was the Gothic Revival of the nineteenth century that brought stained glass back in a big way, but unfortunately little is very good. The situation was improved by the pre-Raphaelites, especially William Morris (1834–96) whose work may be found at Bradford, Dalton and Nun Monkton among other places. Good work was produced by C.E. Kempe (1837–1907) and there is attractive twentieth-century glass in several churches (Adwick-le-Street, Farnley, Wintringham, Wragby and Yarm).

THE NAVE

The main general feature of the nave is the congregational seating or pewing. This is sometimes an unfortunate feature as the general impression may be one of an undifferentiated mass of brown in sharp contrast to the multi-coloured interior of a medieval church. In addition, it may distort the architectural proportions as it almost always conceals the bases and first few feet of any piers in the nave.

Medieval Catholics, like modern Orthodox, generally stood during the services. Nave seating was rare and confined to stone benches built into the foot of the nave wall (an example has survived at Kirkdale), hence the saying 'the weak to the wall'. In the larger church, occasional seats might be provided by raising the bases of the pillars of the arcades (a rare device, perhaps visible at Preston, Humberside).

If the service was unduly prolonged by an extended liturgy (such as those in Holy Week) or additions such as bulls, encyclycals or episcopal letters, the congregation could seek relief by squatting on the straw or reed-covered floor. The wealthy might bring their own cushions or even stools. In the later Middle Ages, increased resources, and perhaps length of sermons, together with a greater desire for comfort, led to naves being increasingly provided with formal, organized seating. This amenity probably first took the form of simple oak benches but, when funds permitted, these were elaborated with supporting backs and, more particularly, with carved end panels. Bench ends were generally rectangular but often had their upper end developed into a vaguely trefoil shape called a poppy-head. This decoration actually bears no resemblance to a poppy, although there are often floral or leafy elements in the design, and the etymology is obscure.

There are few surviving examples of wooden seating from the Middle Ages in Yorkshire and what does remain can scarcely be compared with that of East Anglia and the West Country. Nevertheless, it is worth seeking out if only for its rarity. By far the most complete set of bench ends in the East Riding exists at Hemingborough. They are rectangular, most carved with tracery designs but some with figures of a jester. In addition there are four detached panels with monsters (c. 1520–30) which were once pew ends. At St Michael-le-Belfrey in York there survives a single bench from the early sixteenth century.

In the West Riding there is Perpendicular benchwork at Darrington, Drax, Ecclesfield, and a humble example at Whenby. There are late Perpendicular examples at Rotherham, Sandal Magna and Treeton (the latter have a commemorative inscription dated 1513). The bench ends at Wakefield, Wath and Woolley probably date from the fifteenth century. Sprotborough is furnished with two fine sets of benches, one in the late Perpendicular style and the other, introducing Renaissance motifs, can be dated to the 1550s.

The North Riding survivals are generally rough. These include fifteenth-century bench ends with poppy-heads at Kirby Hill (Boroughbridge), and plain bench ends with trefoil knobs at Marton-in-the-Forest (which date from the fifteenth or sixteenth century). Over Stilton has one sixteenth-century bench end, Raskelf has some crudely carved poppy-heads (late Perpendicular) and there is simple work of an earlier date at South Kilvington. The benches at Wighill have plain ends surmounted by rather coarser poppy-heads.

Sermons were the most important element in post-Reformation services, so pewing was likely to become both more general and more comfortable. The late Perpendicular refurbishing at Sprotborough was completed and brought up to date in the 1550s. Another set, mixing Gothic and Renaissance motifs, exists at Drax and is of about the same date or immediately pre-Reformation. There is also a mixture of styles at Thornton-in-Craven where the square bench ends have tracery panels with two knobs on the top.

There is rare Elizabethan work at Wath-on-Dearne and Elizabethan or Jacobean benches in the north chapel at Waddington. One of the benches at Felkirk has late sixteenth-century inlay. The seats at Stainburn may date from the late sixteenth or early seventeenth centuries.

There are Jacobean benches in a transept at Patrington and one of the simple pews at Kildwick is dated 1624. Bolton Percy has some of 1631, while those at Arksey are coeval with the pulpit of 1634. Leeds St John Briggate has an almost full set of benches, part of the original church furnishings of 1634. Crayke has complete Jacobean pewing: simple, with small decorative panels. The benches at Sinnington are contemporary with the Jacobean altar rails. Wintringham has a Jacobean set which are 'very handsome with their pairs of acorn-like knobs on the top of each end'. The pews at Arksey are of a similar design but the fronts of the first row are open and nicely balustraded. The Jacobean seating at Darfield spreads through both nave and aisles and rises in tiers under the west tower. Pevsner describes the pews at Burneston as 'the most worthwhile thing in the church'. The complete set culminates in the three-tier family pew of Thomas Robinson who paid for the lot in 1627. Leake has a full set of Jacobean benches with small decorative panels. The ends of old Jacobean pews have been used to panel the nave walls at Clapham. Later seventeenth-century pewing exists at Kirk Burton and Barnoldswick, where it is contemporary with the pulpit, as at Stainburn. The fashionable 'bobbin-ended' design can be found in the stalls and benches (c. 1680) at Carlton Husthwaite, neighbouring Husthwaite, Kilburn and Thornton-in-Craven. The benches at Hutton Rudby are of a similar design but decorated only with a single knob. The pews at Wensley probably date from the seventeenth century but their plainness makes them difficult to date more accurately. Those at Dent are partly Jacobean (one dated 1619) and partly of late seventeenth-century design (1693). There are several dated a year later at Bolton-by-Bowland.

The form of seating known as a box pew developed from the seventeenth century. This consisted of a rectangular enclosure, raised to about shoulder height and equipped with benches on three sides. On the fourth side is a door, usually marked to identify the family which rented this private accommodation. Box pews were primarily for middle-class members of the church, falling between the greater family pews nearer the front and the labourers' benches at the back. They continued into the nineteenth century and, though many were demolished as a result of the Anglican revival at the end of that century, they persist in many churches. Kirkby Malham is filled with box pews, dating from the seventeenth to the nineteenth centuries. There is a great collection at Allerton Mauleverer (dating from the seventeenth to eighteenth centuries). Some of the nineteenth century box pews at Silkstone still bear their original owners' names. There are Jacobean examples at Barnoldswick, Bolton Percy and Dent; later seventeenth-century examples at Todwick and Sheriff Hutton; eighteenth-century ones at Harpham, York Holy Trinity Goodramgate and Coxwold; Georgian designs at Burton Agnes, Holme-on-Spalding-Moor, Kirkby Malham, Ruston Parva and Slaidburn; and Victorian examples at York St Michael-le-Belfrey. The old church at Fylingdales, though small, is crammed with box pews all orientated towards the towering three-decker pulpit.

The apogee of pewing in all England must surely be found in St

Mary's, Whitby. Following the Reformation, and with increasing pace during the eighteenth and nineteenth centuries, the appearance of the Norman church was completely transformed as pews multiplied like rabbits. As there was not enough space on the ground floor, galleries were built everywhere to cope with the increasing proliferation. Access was provided by numerous staircases and the loss of light was made good by breaking the ancient walls with sash windows. The demolished rood screen was rather irreverently replaced by Squire Cholmley's elaborate squire's pew in the late seventeenth century. This is white and rises arrogantly on four barley-sugar columns to its parapet crown enriched with putto heads and garlands.

This rather pretentious arrangement at Whitby, however, is rivalled by another, equally arrogant show at Croft. Here the Milbanke family pew (dating from before 1680) is raised like a double box at the theatre, and is even provided with curtains! The structure is supported on substantial Tuscan columns with slimmer ones above and approached by a grand staircase with twisted balusters.

At Boynton the squire was provided with private accommodation in a gallery attached to the west tower which was furnished with a balustrade and convenient staircase. At Burton Agnes the Boynton family acquired suitable seating under a lofty arch framed by Doric pilasters. This Georgian facility is now mutilated although its fireplace was not removed until 1960. There is a complete squire's pew at Tong which still retains its fireplace. External warmth was not the only comfort which the upper class enjoyed in church. Their pews had cupboards for cordials and other refreshments and were well supplied with rugs, cushions and the ministrations of house lackeys. (Weston is provided with 'a family room' equipped with a fireplace and upholstered chairs.)

At Hotham, in the early nineteenth century, a brick extension on the north side of the nave was built to house the squire's pew while, at Sewerby, the neo-Norman church of 1848 was designed to accommodate the squire in the north transept. Later in the century (1876), the former vestry at Knapton was transformed into the squire's pew and given a separate entrance from outside.

Where an ancient family had possessed a chantry chapel in a parish church, this was fairly naturally converted after the Reformation into a family pew. (At Kildwick, the Eltoft family pew of 1633 is located in the former north chapel and that of the Calverleys at Guiseley is in the south.) The powerful Scrope family seem to have cannibalized a very fine rood-screen from Easby Abbey (of which they had been patrons) to supplement the rather coarse woodwork of their pretentious family pew in Wensley, which was erected in the later seventeenth century. On a lesser scale, a family pew in the chancel at Darfield reuses some good pre-Reformation bench ends. Not all family pews were ostentatiously superior to the general provision. At Marske the family pew is simply rather more refined than the accompanying box pews, though Thomas Robinson, who generously supplied pews for the church at Burneston, provided for himself accommodation of a three-tier design crowned by a panel with caryatids and an inscription commemorating his generosity.

Lesser families followed the lead set by the squire and provided themselves with what they considered appropriate seating in their parish church. Skeffling has two such family pews and Kirkby Malham several, one dated 1631. Slaidburn has box pews to the west of the chancel screen and family pews to its east – a survival of the usual Georgian arrangement. There are family pews at Bardsey and Ilkley (1633), an earlier one at Almondbury (1605) and an eighteenth-century squire's pew in the north-west corner of Worsborough.

PULPITS

The provision of pewing was largely related to providing seating for the preacher's audience and, as far as possible, it was therefore directed towards the pulpit. After the Reformation, the pulpit became the focus of the congregation's attention as churches were largely reduced to preaching halls. Church-going, apart from fashion and various kinds of pressure, became mainly a matter of 'sitting under' a preacher. (Preachers' discourses published for reading at home were staples of the book market in the eighteenth and nineteenth centuries.) The importance of the sermon was marked by the increasing dominance of the platform from which it was delivered.

There were, of course, sermons in the Middle Ages – often very popular ones, delivered in the open air by the friars. The average parish priest usually delivered his simple and short homily from the chancel step but many medieval churches were provided with pulpits.

In large churches they were sometimes portable but there were also fixed structures of wood or stone. Few have survived due to natural decay, objection to their 'popish' decoration, or because they have been replaced by what were considered to be more suitable structures.

Medieval pulpits may be found at Edlington, Hickleton, Marr and Rossington. The last dates from the fifteenth century and is exceptionally ornate for Yorkshire.

Perhaps the oldest post-Reformation pulpit is at Rudby-in-Cleveland. It is a rare and pleasant piece, erected as a memorial to Thomas Milner who died in 1594. Braithwaite pulpit is inscribed 1574 and incorporates panels of that date with carved lettering and a kneeling figure. The pulpit at Kirlington has Elizabethan or Jacobean woodwork and is said to be a recycled four-poster bed from the nearby hall.

Jacobean pulpits abound: the one at Halifax may date from as early as 1604. Many are dated: Rotherham, 1604 – 'an exceptionally accomplished piece' with a later Georgian tester; Burnsall and Patrington, 1612; Dent bears the date 1614 but is a largely nineteenth-century reconstruction; Roos, 1615; Swine, 1619; Alne, 1626; Arksey and Halsham, 1634; York All Saints Pavement, 1634; York St Cuthbert and York St Martin-cum-Gregory, both 1636.

More are undated but certainly Jacobean in style. These include examples at Askham Bryan, Bishopestones, Crambe, Hackness, Hauxwell, Nunnington, Osbaldwick, Scalby (which retains an hourglass stand), Stonegrave (which may date from later in the seventeenth century), Walton, Wighill, Wistow, Woodkirk, and York St Denys Walmgate. (Hutton Buscel, Marrick, Seamer, Walton and Wintringham are partly Jacobean.)

The problems of equating style with date are exemplified at Salton where the pulpit looks early Jacobean but was actually made in 1639. Huntington is 'typically Jacobean' but the church was built in 1874. The pulpit at Crayke is dated 1637, at Finghall it comes from the mid-seventeenth century, and there is a very simple seventeenth-century pulpit at Oswaldkirk. The Caroline piece at Aldborough has the inscription, *pasce oves, pasce agnos* (feed my sheep, feed my lambs), and All Saints North St, York has a fine pulpit of 1675. The pulpit at Kilnwick-on-the-Wolds dates from the late seventeenth century as do those at Great Mitton and probably Walkington and Wineshead (with tester). Brodsworth has a well-carved pulpit of 1696 and the one with a tester at Welwick is of the late seventeenth or early eighteenth centuries.

The restrained pulpit at Burton Agnes dates from *c.* 1700 and Routh has a good example of early eighteenth-century work, as has Coxwold. The church register at Methley allows us to date the handsome pulpit there to 1708. The pulpit at Seaton Ross comes from the same century, as does the one at Foston, and Birkin has a handsome eighteenth-century pulpit which is similar to the one at Bolton Percy. Bolton-on-Dearne and Hooton Pagnell have examples with marquetry, while those at Elmley and Wakefield both date from the eighteenth century. The Georgian pulpit at Otley produces markedly different aesthetic responses, while the example at Barwick-in-Elmet, with some inlay, is more generally appreciated. The pulpit at Bolton-by-Bowland includes a nice detached panel from a pulpit of 1703 and its later replacement has applied Flemish reliefs in the Baroque style. Wensley has a pulpit dated 1760 and that at Wragby also bears eighteenth-century work although the decorative panels have been 'brought in' (probably from Italy or Germany). There is a plain 'home-made' piece at Kirkheaton. The pleasant, simple eighteenth-century pulpit at Sutton-on-the-Forest has the additional interest of having once provided the platform from which Laurence Sterne occasionally preached. Middleton has an example with an inlaid tester and Pevsner describes the round, late eighteenth-century pulpit at Pickering as 'very charming'. There is a good, simple pulpit at Kirkleatham which began life as a three-decker, as did the early eighteenth-century one at Romaldkirk which retains the original staircase but the detached lower part is at the west end of the north aisle.

There is a nice, plain early nineteenth-century pulpit at Marske and one dated 1835 (contemporary with the pewing) at Silkstone. Haxby has a High Victorian example of half a century later and there is a pre-Raphaelite gem at Scarborough St Martin (c. 1865). Similar work, designed by Bodley, decorates the pulpit of his heavily restored church at Cawthorne.

The historical survey might conclude with a mention of Downholme which possesses what Collins Guide calls a 'fearsome twentieth-century pulpit'.

Testers or surrounding-boards to improve the acoustic properties of the pulpit seem to have been a late seventeenth-century invention. Testers often represent fine examples of the carpenter's craft, and it is worthwhile noting them when they occur. As well as those mentioned already there are further examples at Arksey, Barwick-in-Elmet, Birkin, Bolton Percy, Deighton, Ellerburn, Emley, Grinton, Holme-on-Spalding-Moor, Husthwaite, Leeds St John Briggate, Lockington, Middleton, Patrington, Rotherham, Sedburgh, Sprotborough (over a pulpit composed of recycled medieval panels), Welwick, Whitby, Winestead and York All Saints Pavement.

Since the pulpit had become the focus of reformed worship, it was judged convenient to attach to it a stall ('reader's desk') to house the minister when he was conducting the service. There are good examples at Carlton Husthwaite, Giggleswick (dated 1680), Ruston Parva, York Holy Trinity Goodramgate and a magnificent piece at Wensley. This produced the so-called double-decker pulpit. A fuller arrangement provided accommodation not only for the minister in his varied functions but also for the parish clerk who was reponsible for leading the congregation's response. (There is, incidentally, an excellent (separate) clerk's desk at Crayke, which dates from the seventeenth century.) This arrangement of reader's desk, preacher's platform and clerk's position became known as the 'three-decker' – standard furniture in Anglican churches of the eighteenth and nineteenth centuries (even the tiny 18 ft long chapel at Lead had one crammed into a corner). There are other survivals at Barnoldswick, in the old churches at Fylingdales and Great Ayton, Romaldkirk (dismembered), Slaidburn, Tong, Weston and Whitby.

The pulpit was equipped with a small lectern to hold the preacher's notes, candles to read by when natural light failed and a sand-glass to mark the hours of the discourse. The 'full set' of pulpit fitments rarely survives but there are remains of hour-glass stands at Croft, Keyingham, Scalby and a rare survival of the glass itself at South Kilvington.

The minister's reading-desk, often attached to the pulpit, may be provided as a separate item. The modern piece at Sprotborough, although separate, was designed to match the earlier work. There is Jacobean work at Bolton Percy and Wintringham, seventeenth-century work at Riccal, eighteenth-century work at Kirkleatham and modern, twentieth-century pieces at Little Ouseburn (incorporating medieval panels) and Foston (decorated with a pelican).

Associated furniture might include the Litany desk. This is a priedieu or kneeling-desk, used for prayer, facing east as distinct from the west-facing reading-desk, and there is a very rich example at Leeds St Aidan.

LECTERN

The pulpit stands on the north side of the nave – a relic of medieval symbolism where the north represents heathendom to which the Gospel was to be proclaimed. (The Gospel at mass was read at the north side of the altar. Medieval stone lecterns for this purpose survive at Paull and Ottringham.) Opposite, on the south side, usually stands a large lectern to support the Bible from which lessons are read at Morning and Evening Prayer.

Very rarely, pulpit and lectern are designed as a matching pair, and there is an eighteenth-century example at Denton. This arrangement is reminiscent of the ancient basilican practice of providing two outward-facing pulpits, called 'ambos', in the west wall of the chancel screen. Examples of this survive on the Continent, perhaps the most famous at St Clement's in Rome.

A lectern actually in the nave seems to have been an Anglican innovation and the preferred later form is a great brass stand terminating in an eagle with outspread wings on which the Bible is supported. The design is actually medieval: one dating from *c.* 1500 survives in Southwell Cathedral. Together with some fine brass candlesticks, this lectern was discovered in the former fish-pond of Newstead Abbey into which they were thrown when the monastery was dissolved.

These large medieval lecterns stood in the quire to support the heavy music books used by the cantors. When books of Bible readings were required away from the altar, they were carried into position by a minor cleric who then held them up for the officiant to read. There are rare survivals of medieval lecterns modified for Anglican use. All Saints Pavement, York has a greatly altered fifteenth-century example in oak which originally belonged to St Crux. Bilton Ainstey has a much restored wooden eagle originally dating from the late fifteenth or early sixteenth centuries. Possibly, the finest example is the spectacular metal lectern at Methley, probably Dutch work of *c.* 1500. It is a delicate and highly skilful piece of craftsmanship with architectural and figurative elements. It was presented to the church in 1869 with an added eagle-top of this later period.

Another piece from the Netherlands is the late seventeenth-century lectern at Rosedale. There are putti and foliage on the foot and the reading-desk is supported on an angel's wing.

Almondbury has an early Georgian gilded eagle which Pevsner thinks was perhaps made for another purpose. There is an eighteenth-century wooden lectern in the Beaumont Chapel at Kirkheaton and Wragby has an imported piece of the same period which is probably Flemish in origin.

There is an elaborate brass lectern of 1847 at Hull parish church while the nineteenth-century example at Boynton provides an unusual variation. The usual eagle is replaced by a turkey, apparently to commemorate the introduction of this bird into the country by Sir William Strickland in the late sixteenth century. Another curiosity exists at Thornton Watless where the lectern incorporates the figure-head of a ship. There is a successful twentieth-century design at Brandsby.

AISLES, SIDE ALTARS, SQUINTS

Before leaving the area of the nave, one might look for extensions. These usually consist of aisles (from the Latin word for 'wing') and are built to provide extra accommodation. If the church was not originally designed with aisles, the first move was to pierce the south wall by an arcade, build a new, lower external wall and connect the two by a sloping roof. If even more room was required, the same procedure was carried out on the north side of the nave.

Such extensions were often separated by a considerable period of time and this is often represented by the different architectural designs of the two arcades. It may be interesting to note whether the arcades are extended westwards to embrace the tower (as at Bardsey) or eastwards to flank the chancel.

The building of a south aisle normally affected the main entrance and a valuable Norman door was sometimes moved to serve in a new position (this happened at Goldsborough). Such changes could be avoided by stopping the aisle short of the south door as is the case at Kildwick.

A single aisle might have provided all that was needed and therefore a further one was never built, leaving the church with a lop-sided appearance, as the church at High Melton. The parochial nave at Bolton Abbey could not be provided with a south aisle because of the pre-existing monastic cloister.

A dominant motive in the provision of aisles, however, was not so much to create additional congregational space as to provide room for more altars – a Lady chapel, for example. This devotion developed greatly in the thirteenth century but the Lady chapels at Silkstone and Ecclesfield were not endowed until 1514 and 1533 respectively. (The word 'chapel' (from the Latin 'capella' – a cloak) originated from the small sacred edifice built at Tours, probably in the fifth century, to house the venerated relic of St Martin's cloak.)

A feature of town churches was the addition of Guild chapels for these proliferating and increasingly powerful medieval institutions. The South 'aisle' at Scarborough, for example, consists entirely of four chapels of varying sizes, added in the late fourteenth century.

Guild chapels were 'private' chapels. They were built, furnished and supplied with a priest at the expense of the guild. (Apart from the formal guilds, there were looser parochial fraternities of a pious and benevolent nature who often provided furnishings (especially lights) and occasionally had their own chapel within the parish church.)

Chantry chapels were even more private in that they were provided for the prime benefit of a single family which built and endowed them so that requiem masses might be perpetually sung there for their (and others') good estate in the after-life. They frequently provided a burial place for their founder and other members of the family, often in a recessed tomb in the wall (see, for instance, the Marmion chapel at West Tanfield). The chaplains of these chapels, because of their light priestly duties, sometimes also functioned as schoolmasters.

Chantries were largely a fourteenth-century fashion and their chapels were usually attached to the end of north aisles. Such chapels founded in Yorkshire included Bolton and Wath (1322), Todwick (1328), Owston and Goldsborough (with founder's tomb, 1333) and Skelbrook (1388). There were later (and more ostentatious) additions at Loversall (c. 1530) and Kirk Sandal (c. 1525).

The brass to William Burgh (†1492) in the North chapel at Catterick describes him as 'the founder of this chantry'. So does that to Robert Thirsk (†1419) whose chantry was licensed in 1431. Its construction initiated the entire rebuilding of Thirsk parish church.

The will of Sir Robert Waterton of Methley (†1424) requested that his body should be buried in Methley church and that a chantry chapel (for the erection of which he left £200) should be built alongside the chancel on the north side.

For some reason, the work of building the chapel alongside the chancel was delayed for some sixty years and it was not until the beginning of the sixteenth century that the three endowed priests could begin to carry out Sir Robert's intention that they should sing soul masses for ever in the Waterton chapel. The chantry priests no longer sing but there remains an exceptionally fine carved tomb with effigies of Sir Robert and his wife in alabaster.

The first stages of the Reformation had actually begun when the south chapel of Osmotherley was built in accordance with the will of

Sir James Strangeways (†1540) 'to make an aisle' on the south side of the quire for the burial of himself and his wife.

Though they needed the bishop's licence for their erection, these chantry chapels were substantially private property and after the Reformation they often became a family chapel, family pew or mausoleum. Some mausolea were erected in the graveyard or in the grounds of the family mansion (as, for example, at Castle Howard, built 1731–42). The massive Turner mausoleum was attached to the north side of the chancel at Kirkleatham in 1740.

The status of possessing a private chapel continued and developed after the Reformation. At Lockington, the Estofts converted the south chapel to family use in the early seventeenth century when it was panelled and decorated with over 170 armorial shields (renovated in 1851). A similar appropriation took place at Rowley in 1730 and at Winestead rather more than a century earlier where the Hillyards built and decorated a chapel to house their family monuments of which the earliest dates from 1602. The octagonal Frankland chapel at Thirkelby was built in 1850.

In the Middle Ages, subordinate chapels were separated from the main body of the church by screens. In major churches (Howden, Hull and Selby, for example) and in some others (Harewood and Methley), these are of stone but, more commonly, they are made of wood and are known as parclose screens. Earlier wooden screens (if they existed) were, like much else, generally replaced in the Perpendicular period (Decorated work remains at Kirk Ella). Perpendicular screens have survived in many places, of which the following are a small selection: Batley, Ecclesfield, Fishlake, Hemingborough, Kirk Sandal, Silkstone, Swine.

A further type of screen was the western screen, which was sometimes provided to divide the open ground floor of a tower from the nave. The western screen at Wintringham is dated 1723 and combines Classical with Gothic elements. That at Throapham is in the Perpendicular style.

The desire for privacy led to the renewal of screens around what were now family chapels. The Elizabethan screen of the Sherburne chapel at Mitton, for example, contains fifteenth-century tracery. There is Jacobean work on a screen at Stillingfleet and a late seventeenth-century piece at Methley. The early Renaissance panels functioning as a screen to the north chapel at Kirkby Wharfe come from the furnishings of a house, while the screen to the south chapel at Bawtry is a fine eighteenth-century wrought-iron garden gate.

Sometimes the addition of minor altars necessitated the provision of a squint (or, as pedantic nineteenth-century ecclesiologists named it, a 'hagioscope'). This was an opening, giving a view of the High Altar from a minor altar, so that the celebrant at the latter might be aware of the progress of the principal mass and would not begin his own mass at some inconvenient moment. (There are examples of squints at Birkin, Conisbrough, Low Catton, Romaldkirk, and a remarkably long one at Thwing.)

These devices were sometimes created as a result of changes made elsewhere in the church building. Squints became necessary at West Tanfield, for instance, when the chancel was widened. Sometimes existing arrangements were altered to serve the purpose, as at Scawton where original niches were modified into squints.

In rare cases, squints provided a view of the altar from outside the church. The squint near the priest's door at Kirkburton is said to have originally opened from a now demolished anchorite's cell.

Such cells could form another kind of extension to the nave, and there are examples in the north-west corner of Skipton, and at the west end of the north aisle at Riccall. Chantries could also provide additional space in the nave, as shown by the unique extension in the south wall of the north chapel at West Tanfield (though this belongs to the chancel rather than to the nave).

THE CHANCEL-ARCH

In medieval symbolism, the nave represented earthly life while the chancel foreshadowed heaven with its white-clothed figures singing God's praises. The chancel-arch was the division between them and thus could be seen as the gate of heaven and consequently worthy of rich ornamentation by carving and colour.

Limited building skills prevented the elaboration of Anglo-Saxon arches, such as those at Hackness, Kirkdale, Kirk Hammerton and Ledsham, but this deficiency was more than made good by the Norman masons. The most famous example in Yorkshire is the sumptuous chancel-arch at Adel, ornamented with beak-heads, box-frames and zigzag. The capitals (head or top part of the column) portray the baptism of Christ on the north and His crucifixion on the south. Other sculptures include beasts, a centaur archer, and a mounted lancer. (The fact that the carving on the east side has not been completed to match that on the west side suggests, incidentally, that such sculptural detail was done *in situ* and not before the structure was assembled.)

Birkin has a tall chancel-arch with much zigzag, and there is a similar, but heavily restored, example at Kilburn. The arch at Scawton is unusually plain but interesting for its side niches, designed to support the reredoses of flanking altars but later converted into squints.

The unusual structure of the Norman chancel-arch at Healaugh argues that it was once incorporated into a low stone screen. Bugthorpe provides a curiosity. There are two chancel-arches because a rebuilding scheme of *c.* 1300 was not completed, leaving the new Early English arch as well as the earlier Norman one. The capitals of the latter are most interesting, though some detail is lost through the heavy whitewashing. They have small carvings of Christ in an almond-shaped glory, Peter with his keys, a mermaid and decorative trails.

The chancel-arch at Bishop Wilton is large, wide and high with rich decoration in the arch itself (carefully restored in 1859).

The beauty of later chancel-arches lies more in their line than in surface decoration and this may be deliberate, to avoid distracting the eye from other features which were developing at the junction of nave and chancel.

According to Christian theology, heaven could only be reached from earth by way of the redeeming death of Christ on the cross and the flat surface of the wall above and about the chancel-arch was used to underline this teaching. The area was plastered and then painted with a representation of the last judgement or perhaps of the crucifixion. This 'infilling' was called a tympanum (as is the similar shaped space over a door), and supports for the (wooden) framework can be seen in the chancel-arches at Hornsea and Pocklington. A modern version exists in the great crucifix over the chancel-arch at Thirsk.

More frequently, a three-dimensional image of the crucifix (for which the Anglo-Saxon word is 'rood') was carried on a great beam which stretched across the entrance to the chancel. Such rood-beams rarely survived the Reformation (there are none in Yorkshire) but one or more of the corbels (projections placed high on the nave walls to carry its weight), which once supported it, can sometimes be discerned and occasionally the beam itself has been reintroduced (for example, at St Wilfrid, Harrogate, and Kirby Underdale).

Churches always had a clear demarcation between nave and chancel; in the early basilicas it was the open-work screen (cancelli) which gave its name to the latter. The screen existed in English churches (we have seen indications at Healaugh) and was sometimes raised to a considerable height (as are the remains at Laughton-en-le-Morthen). In great churches (where it is called a pulpitum) it entirely blocks the chancel from view (Beverley, Ripon, York Minsters). The stone panels now forming a reredos at Hedon were originally part of the pulpitum.

The normal practice in parish churches was to provide an elaborate screen of wood (called the rood-screen because of the crucifix which rose from its top). These masterly examples of the carpenter's craft naturally vary in detail but have a common basic design.

They consist of an unequal number of bays (usually five), the central one being wider to accommodate the doorway. The lower half is panelled (originally painted, usually with representations of saints), while the upper part is open-work, rising to vaults which support the loft on which stood the 'Great Rood' flanked by figures of St Mary and St John. The loft is comparatively wide: sufficient to allow access to the rood and the lights which burned before it. In great churches it could accommodate a small altar and sometimes an organ. The whole is normally embellished with rich tracery and foliage-trains (usually wheat and vine). Originally, the entire structure was brightly coloured and gilded to provide an eye-catching symbolic and aesthetic feature.

Surviving medieval screens generally date from the Perpendicular period, a time when much of the increasing wealth of the country was being expended on the building and improvement of churches of every kind. (There is a rare survival of Decorated work at Kirk Ella.) Old furniture was replaced by more lavish and up-to-date work and the font cover and chancel-screen offered particular opportunities for the laity to express their devotion and generosity by providing spectacular nave furniture.

In the medieval parish church the laity generally provided chancel- or rood-screens of whatever richness they could afford, but these never escaped reforming zeal. The rood was always destroyed and often significantly replaced by the Royal Arms. The treatment of the substructure varied from complete demolition to less thorough destruction and, in more stable times, some were restored or replaced.

Fairly substantial medieval remains of rood-screens exist in a few places. One of the best Yorkshire survivals, which was recovered, restored and re-erected in 1881, is at Burghwallis. There are other good examples at nearby Campsall and Owston. The former is similar to the screen at Hatfield and bears a rhymed inscription which, enigmatically, advises the reader to 'Beware the Devil when he blows his horn'. The screen at Owston, unlike Burghwallis, retains its doors, while the Hatfield screen, like Campsall, retains the coving of the loft.

The rood-screen at Flamborough, though much restored, is the most complete in the East Riding and still has its parapet furnished with (empty) canopied niches. The only surviving loft in the West Riding is at Hubberholme. It is dated 1558 and thus represents a Marian restoration (though there is some evidence that it is the wrong way round, as the more decorated side faces the altar rather than the nave!). The Skipton screen appears to have been erected comparatively late in the reign of Henry VIII (1533).

There are further substantial screen remains at Crayke (much restored), Ecclesfield, Great Mitton, Patrington, Sprotborough, Sutton (Humberside), Welwick, Winestead, Worsborough, and a humble example at Whenby. The screen at Swine (1531) is interesting as it shows the beginnings of Renaissance style. Even more interesting is the example at Hornby which retains the only substantial Yorkshire evidence of screen painting. This consists not of the usual figures as the main motif, but of naturalistic designs, mostly birds in thick foliage.

Elsewhere, screen remains are more fragmentary, often only the dado cut down to the level of the return stalls in the chancel (as at Bolton Percy). But even fragments may be worth a close look. Part of the cornice beam which survives at Pickhill has human heads, and hare and hounds.

Often the only evidence of a former rood-screen lies in the remains of the staircase which once gave access to its loft. It is often cunningly contrived in the wall or pier to the north of the screen's site. The remarkable example at Darrington is enclosed in a vast fifteenth-century stair-turret from which the loft is reached via a small arcaded gallery over the north aisle.

The convenience and propriety of a division between nave and chancel became realized after the first Protestant fury had passed and post-Reformation screens of various styles and periods were reintroduced.

The mural tablet to Emma Louisa Catherine Slingsby (†1899) at St John, Knaresborough, North Yorkshire

The Gascoigne brass at St Helen, Burghwallis, South Yorkshire. The figure depicts Sir Thomas Gascoigne, †1544

A late twelfth-century (restored) pillar type piscina at St Peter, Conisbrough, South Yorkshire. (Note the squint opening above.)

A thirteenth-century piscina at St Peter, Bradford, West Yorkshire

The fine black marble font, c. 1412, at St Anne, Catterick, North Yorkshire

The Elizabethan font cover at St Andrew, Slaidburn (formerly West Riding, now Lancashire)

Sir William Gascoigne, Lord Chief Justice, and his wife, Elizabeth Mowbray, c. 1419, at All Saints, Harewood, West Yorkshire

Sir Richard Redman, c. 1426, also at All Saints, Harewood

Heraldic glass, c. 1800, at St James, High Melton, South Yorkshire

The unique oriel window on the great Perpendicular tower of St John Baptist, Royston, South Yorkshire

The post-Reformation eighteenth-century pulpit at St Helen, Denton, West Yorkshire

A carved bench end in the nave at St Mary, Hemingbrough, North Yorkshire

The early thirteenth-century east window at St Peter, East Marton, North Yorkshire

The apsidal transept, c. 1928, at St Wilfrid, Harrogate, North Yorkshire

The remains of four wooden panels, probably bench ends, at St Mary, Hemingbrough, North Yorkshire

Screenwork at St Peter, Barnbrough, South Yorkshire

There is an excellent Jacobean example at Slaidburn and an even better one at Seamer (1637). The very sumptuous and extensive screen at Leeds St John Briggate dates from 1634, a year earlier than the exceptionally fine piece at Wakefield (now cathedral). Though it has lost its dado to provide a reredos elsewhere in the church, the screen at Stonegrave (1637) remains attractive. Wighill has a low division between nave and chancel which is little more than an advanced communion rail (probably 1670–80).

The eighteenth-century screen at Boynton is virtually a doubled chancel-arch. That at Bempton is described by Hutchinson as 'unique in Yorkshire' (Pevsner, p.168). It dates either from the late eighteenth century or possibly from the 1829 restoration of the church. It consists of three elliptical arches rising from tall, fluted pillars and has panelling above which incorporates the Royal Arms.

The quiet, dignified interior of the the mid-nineteenth-century church of St Hilda at Whitby is furnished with a high screen topped by a rood. There is a serious essay in the Gothic style by Temple Moore at Pockley (1889) and the restored rood has figures by Lang of Oberammergau. The same architect has provided a conventionally Gothic screen at Kirkby Moorside (1919). In contrast, one might cite the remarkable piece in brass and iron by Street at Bishop Wilton and the fine rood-screen by Comper at High Melton. Kirby Sigston provides a twentieth-century example of a rood-screen.

Besides those mentioned above, there are several other examples of restored roods by known designers. These include roods at Beverley St Mary (by Oldrid Scott), Womersley (by Bodley), Hull St Mary and Roos (by Temple Moore), Beighton (by Comper), Nether Poppleton (by H. Harvey), Bolton-on-Dearne (by A. Dearne).

QUIRE

Beyond the chancel-screen lies the quire where, in the Middle Ages, the seven daily offices were sung. Of these, Mattins (the early morning service) and Vespers (or Evensong) were often attended by parishioners. Seats (stalls) were provided for the clergy and choir. The former sat facing the altar and with their backs to the screen (in the return stalls) while the latter faced each other across the quire aisle. (The particularly fine return stalls, with small figures in the front of the bench-ends, at Ecclesfield are built into the rood-screen.)

Quire seating became increasingly elaborate, especially in the churches which were staffed by a 'college' of clerics. Such churches were known as collegiate churches, and could be great minsters or a village church such as Hemingborough which was made collegiate in 1426.

In a large church, the quire was lofty and often flanked by aisles. These features added excessive draughts to the normally cold conditions of an unheated building. Where funds permitted, comfort was improved by adding backs or screens to the choir stalls and canopies overhead (often of remarkable complexity).

Long services with elaborate music could be tiring, especially if they took place late at night or very early in the morning. This led to the invention of the misericord (the word basically means 'relief'). This was a tip-up seat so designed that, when raised, its upper edge could give some support even when its occupant was standing.

The supporting bracket, though usually concealed, provided an opportunity for the medieval carver to show his skill. His scope was greatest in the extensive quires of the minsters (Beverley has sixty-eight surviving misericords, Ripon has thirty-five) but there were opportunities elsewhere (Beverley St Mary has twenty-three carved between 1425 and 1450). Hackness has 14 although half of them are plain, while Wakefield retains 10 original examples, Halifax 9 and Old Malton (originally a Gilbertine priory) 8 – the same number as the former Cistercian nunnery at Swine. Richmond preserves twelve rescued from the destruction of Easby Abbey.

Only one remains at Hemingborough but it is probably the oldest in England, dating from the thirteenth century, and significantly antedates the church's elevation to collegiate status by some two centuries. There are other sole survivors at Middleton and at York in All Saints North St. and St Mary Castlegate. There are two in Loversall, Rotherham and Saviours, York. Three survive at Sprotborough and four at Darrington.

The subject-matter of misericord carving is fascinating and derives from natural forms, grotesqueries, heraldry, humour and satire, religious symbols, fables and scenes of everyday life, not to mention images whose significance has been lost.

The design of stalls themselves is worth examination for the solution of such problems as spacing, the junction of the return stalls with the main seating, etc. The quality is always good but it can vary from the simple to the elaborate. There are two splendid stall ends at Leake and a pair of similar ones at Over Stilton. This similarity seems to indicate that they belonged to the same set which probably once graced a northern religious house before its dissolution.

There are also parallels between the stall ends at Aysgarth, Hauxwell and Wensley which were carved in the early sixteenth century and probably all represent the work of the same carpenter. South Cowton has stalls with poppy-heads and other ornament; those at Woodkirk have architectural decoration and poppy-heads; and there are fifteenth-century choir stalls at Rotherham.

All medieval services were sung: the seven daily offices and the various masses (including the more or less solitary requiem in the private chantry – hence its name). The Reformation changed this, however, as organs came under the epithet of 'popish' and were usually destroyed or, if of the small portable sort, expropriated.

The Elizabethan musical Renaissance seems to have encouraged the singing of anthems in some churches but this was not formalized until 1662 when the Anglican prayer-book was re-introduced after the Commonwealth. Then, in the offices of Morning and Evening Prayer, before the final petitions, the following rubric was inserted: 'In Quires and Places where they sing, here follows the Anthem'.

Cathedrals led the way with great music by Purcell, Handel and others, but by the end of the eighteenth century simple parish churches were acquiring rustic choirs accompanied by the village band in lieu of an organ. They seem usually to have been accommodated in a gallery built at the west end of the church. The gallery at St Michael-le-Belfrey, York, is adorned with the Royal Arms on its front (1785) and there is a good west gallery at Kirkby-in-Cleveland. There are other eighteenth-century examples at Bishopestones (1705?), Burghwallis (possibly), Holme-on-Spalding-Moor (1767), Coxwold, Danby, Langthwaite, Nether Poppleton and Sowerby. There are nineteenth-century examples at Hinderwell and Fylingdales. The later nineteenth-century Anglican 'Counter-Reformation' replaced the choir in its traditional position and many useless west galleries were dismantled. Sometimes their material was recycled. The west screen at Lockington and pews at Burton Agnes are constructed of such recycled material.

The return of the choir to the chancel usually necessitated the replacement of their stalls, consequently most are undistinguished work of the later nineteenth-century and after. The stalls at South Kilvington were carved by the rector and there are good modern choir stalls (1950) at Sutton-on-the-Forest. Throughout North

Yorkshire there are examples of fine work by Thompson of Kilburn –
the 'mouse man' – such as the communion rail and pews at Wycliffe.

SANCTUARY/PRESBYTERY

The destruction of the chancel-screen in the first excesses of the
Reformation laid open the entire area beyond, resulting in various
unwanted intrusions – dogs, for example, who found the legs of the
new communion tables attractive.

Queen Elizabeth I thought some dignity should be restored to the
ravaged churches, including some indication of their religious
purpose. The first protection of the area around the communion table
dates from her reign but it was mainly in the subsequent period that
communion rails began to be part of the normal furniture of the
chancel.

Those at Leake seem to have made use of old parts of the former
rood-screen but normally they were specially, and well, made. There
are Jacobean examples at Askham Bryan, Austerfield, Cowthorpe,
Darfield, Edstone, Kirkby Malham, Marton-in-the-Forest, Monk
Fryston, Normanby (North Riding), Sheriff Hutton, Sinnington,
Sprotborough and Wighill.

Later seventeenth-century work appears at Carlton Husthwaite
(1698), Croft, Cowesby, East Harsley, Giggleswick (1676), Halifax
(1698), Kirby Sigston, Todwick, Osbaldwick, Watton and Wensley.

The communion rails at Otley and Gillamoor are dated c. 1700 and
those at Raskelf also appear to belong to the turn of the century.
There is early eighteenth-century work at Darton, York St Martin-
cum-Gregory, and the rail at Harpham is dated 1726. Seaton Ross,
Patrick Brompton, Harthill (and possibly Aldborough) possess
eighteenth-century pieces and a fine example of the Georgian style
exists at Kirkleatham.

The usual way of defining the altar area was by a straight rail from
one wall of the chancel to the other, set back a little way east of the
step which was the normal medieval demarcation of the presbytery.
An alternative was to enclose the communion table on three sides, the
so-called 'pen' type of railing (there is a fine early eighteenth-century
example at York St Michael Spurriergate and a nineteenth-century
example at Ottringham). This was sometimes elaborated to increase
the accommodation for communicants by developing the centre

portion into a westward semi-circular projection (there are two examples in York: St Michael-le-Belfrey and Holy Trinity Goodramgate 1721).

A unique form of communion rail survives at Coxwold where a long tongue stretches west from a 'pen' beginning. This is caused by the intrusion of the Bellasis monuments into the chancel which leaves little space for religious activity.

There is a fine communion rail of metal (1908) at Selby.

SEDILIA

The medieval altar area naturally included seating for the ministers of the altar: the priest and his assistants. At first, this was a simple bench and/or a collection of stools, and wooden seating for the clergy remained the norm in minor chapels. (A rare fifteenth-century oak bench survives at Sheffield Cathedral, the former parish church of SS Peter and Paul.)

Movable wooden seating round the high altar was replaced by stone at an early date and inevitably when the chancel was rebuilt (as it often was in the thirteenth century and later). The earliest stone seats (sedilia) were similar to the wooden benches with roughly carved arms at either end (as at Burghwallis, Owston and Spennithorne).

The thirteenth century saw the introduction of more elaborate designs. There is a fine Early English example at Filey and other examples at Easby (with surviving painted decoration) and Wensley.

The development continued in the Decorated style of the early fourteenth century, at such places as Burstwick, Drayton (renewed), Kirk Smeaton, Langtoft, Patrington, Patrick Brompton (an original design), Pickering, Rudston and South Anston. The nineteenth-century church at Kirby Moorside retains fourteenth-century sedilia as does the rebuilt church at Topcliffe.

There are Perpendicular sedilia at Burneston (with crocketed gables), Catterick and Thirsk (c. 1470), and remains of such at Stokesley.

Sedilia usually provide accommodation for three ministers, the priest, deacon and subdeacon of a high mass. However, the number of places can vary: the stone throne or armchair at Thornton Steward, and the early fourteenth-century sedile at Burstwick accommodate one; the sedile at Scawton now has room for only one but it was originally designed for two; the bench at Spennithorne is a two-seater, while the Decorated sedilia at Skipton have places for four.

It is interesting to compare the elaborate provision in some churches with the simple expedient at Swine.

PISCINA

The most characteristic furniture in the vicinity of a medieval altar is the piscina. Indeed it is often now the only indication that there was once an altar nearby.

The word 'piscina' originally meant fish-pond, then pool, and then water-basin, and finally came to be used for this item of church equipment. Basically it is a drain for the reverent disposal of water which has been in contact with holy things.

Pope Leo IV (AD 847–55) was probably only applying uniformity to a variety of pious practices when he decreed that a drain should be made near every altar for the disposal of the water in which the sacred vessels were rinsed at the end of mass. (The idea was that the water should be conducted into hallowed ground: either the churchyard or the church's foundations.)

An early solution was to insert a stone with a bowl-shaped depression and central drain-hole in the floor. A number of these survive in the ruins of Yorkshire abbeys. A more convenient solution was to raise the bowl on a short pillar with a hole bored down its centre, producing the 'pillar piscina'. This was a fairly common provision in Norman parish churches. Survivals, however, are rare but see Barton-le-Street, Easinton, Foston (displaced?), Sherburn, Adel (ejected), Hinderwell (bowl only) and a thirteenth-century example at Conisborough.

The preferred form was to set the piscina, at a convenient height, in an arched recess whence the water could drain through the wall into the ground below. There are survivals of this form of piscina from all periods, and an unusual square-headed example at Kirby Ravensworth. The arches are usually enriched with the architectural ornament of the time (see examples at Sinnington (Norman), Scawton, Kirby Grindalhythe (Early English), Barnby Dun (an unusual Decorated design), Goxhill, Ripley, Walton (Perpendicular style)).

A further enactment in the thirteenth century required the priest to wash his hands (after censing) and before beginning the Canon (central prayer of mass). A second piscina was added for the disposal of this water, thus producing the 'double piscina'. In the fourteenth century, the custom arose of the priest drinking the water used for the cleansing of the vessels and so there was a reversion to the single piscina. (This means that 'double piscinas' can be dated to the later thirteenth or earlier fourteenth centuries: fine examples exist at Romaldkirk and South Anston.)

There are several unusual and even mysterious piscina designs: the 'angle' form (at Darrington, for example); the curious stone at the back of the piscina at Bowes; and the 'super piscina' at Scawton.

Many piscinas were fitted with a shelf in the upper part of the niche, as at Sprotborough. Even if the shelf is missing, the grooves for its support sometimes survive. The shelf was used to accommodate the cruets which contained the wine and water used at mass. A small amount of water was added to the wine in the chalice before it was blessed. (It was the custom in the classical world to add water to wine before drinking it and it is assumed that Christ followed this temperate practice.) The water was also used to wash (symbolically) the priest's hands. The support for these vessels was called the credence. Modern practice is to use a small table, covered with a linen cloth, on which are placed the containers for the bread, wine and water, a small basin and finger-towel. There are curious early fourteenth-century stone tables at Hemingborough and Pocklington which may be credences but they seem too substantial for this purpose.

The word 'credence' is derived from the Latin 'credo' and its ecclesiastical use seems to have developed from its application to any side-table on which food was placed for tasting or in readiness for serving.

When a chancel was rebuilt, the piscina was usually associated with the sedilia in an overall and satisfying design. Perhaps the finest examples are at Beverley St Mary and Patrington. There are many others, however, including a late thirteenth-century set at Dunnington and a fifteenth-century one at Bolton Percy. (Several others are mentioned under 'sedilia'.) The 'set' at Croft includes an aumbry (see overleaf) and is an extremely ambitious thirteenth-century design although rather crudely executed. That at Kirby Wiske (c. 1300) includes a rare Easter Sepulchre (see overleaf).

EASTER SEPULCHRE

The Easter Sepulchre was used in the celebrations of the last days of Holy Week and provided a receptacle in which a representation of the body of Christ was placed from the afternoon of Good Friday until the dawn of Easter Day. It was located on the north side of the chancel and an existing table-tomb may have provided the base for a temporary or movable structure. There is an extremely rare survival of a fifteenth-century wooden Easter Sepulchre at Cowthorpe.

In some cases, the Easter Sepulchre was a built-in architectural feature of the north wall of the chancel. Roche Abbey has the remains of an elaborate and richly decorated structure of this kind.

When the church at Owston was provided with a new chancel at about the end of the thirteenth century, the opportunity was taken to build in a fine Easter Sepulchre. It consists of the sort of recess that was used to contain an important tomb, cusped and with a crocketed gable. The interior recess continues to roof level, presumably to carry away the fumes from the many candles that would have surrounded the sepulchre when it was in use. This type of survival seems unique but there is a more common design at Patrington (similar to some in Lincolnshire). It is in three tiers with a representation of the tomb guard in the lowest panel and, above, the recess for the sepulchre (c. 1350). West Heslerton has a less elaborate example dating from the late thirteenth century, and there is an earlier one at Kirby Wiske. A large recess in the north wall of the chancel at Patrick Brompton may be the remains of an Easter Sepulchre.

AUMBRIES

Aumbries are cupboards, often made of wood. More secure ones were often provided in recesses in the church wall, closed by a lockable door which was recessed into the stonework. Sometimes the recess is L-shaped, providing much more interior space than is first apparent.

Aumbries near altars were usually for the safe custody of the valuable altar vessels but they may serve other purposes. The mechanism that lowered the pyx (vessel in which consecrated bread was kept) over the high altar was sometimes secured within an aumbry, or the aumbry itself might contain the reserved sacrament (the aumbry in the south wall of the chancel at Swine has been refurbished to serve this purpose). The aumbry in the north wall at

Scawton (possibly originating as an Easter Sepulchre) was restored in the seventeenth century. Sometimes the Holy Oils were secured within an aumbry (this is probably the purpose of the one at Croft, unusually placed at the west end, near the font). The aumbry which originally served a chapel in the transept at Wath is equipped with a shelf. The chancel aumbry at Foston has, as its back panel, a curious slab of plaster decorated with bands and pairs of birds. It may date from the twelfth century but poses something of a mystery.

THE ALTAR

The high (or chief) altar is not only the focus of the chancel, but the *raison d'etre* of the church itself. Its hallowing was the centre-piece of a church's consecration.

The medieval altar consisted of a monolithic stone slab (mensa) raised on a solid stone base or piers. The mensa was seen as a symbol of Christ, the corner-stone, and was marked with five crosses to represent His wounds. Associations with the catacombs (and perhaps the influence of Rev. 6:9) led to the placing of relics of the saints under the mensa or in a sealed cavity in its surface or front edge.

The 'catacomb experience' also led to the building of churches with their altar over the underground tomb of a martyr (for example, the Roman basilicas of St Peter, St Paul, St Laurence and so on). This, in turn, led to the provision of crypts to provide more convenient access to the relics of the saint. This practice spread throughout the Western Church.

The oldest crypt in Yorkshire is that built by St Wilfrid for his minster at Ripon, *c.* 700. Another remarkable survival is the one built *c.* 1080 at Lastingham to house the remains of St Cedd. It is a prodigious structure, forming an underground church complete with apse.

Other survivals are few, less remarkable and not always accessible, but they exist, for instance, at Bedale, Doncaster, Halifax, Horbury, Hornsea (with fireplace!), Stanley, Thirsk and York St Cuthbert.

The word 'altar' implies sacrifice (OT passim and Heb. 12:10) and the word was commonly used of the Eucharistic table at least from the beginning of the second century. Because it was the place where Christ's institution was reiterated, it was always highly venerated and richly adorned, sometimes even being covered with gold plates.

The medieval altar was given visual prominence by being raised on a step and by being surrounded on three sides by curtains of the richest material that could be afforded. Increasingly, the curtain backing the altar (dossal) was replaced by a carved, coloured and gilded panel of wood or stone (alabaster was a favourite material because it was soft enough to take detailed carving). This was called a reredos.

Hovingham retains a stone panel (c. 800) which may once have formed the reredos (or perhaps frontal) of an Anglo-Saxon altar. Detached alabaster panels from former reredoses survive at Burnsall, Ripon and Selby. There are fragments of two reredoses (still with traces of colour) at Preston (Humberside) and a damaged reredos of the Decorated period survives at Darfield.

Because of its associations with the sacrifice of the mass, a doctrine which the extreme reformers particularly abominated, the medieval altars became a special focus of their furious destruction. They were not only smashed but often deliberately profaned (for example, by using the mensas as paving stones so that they would be necessarily trodden underfoot).

The destroyed altar was replaced by the more theologically acceptable communion table of domestic type. A growing sense of propriety in the Jacobean period produced more worthy bespoke furniture and some of these tables are still in use in the sanctuary, though others have been demoted to serve elsewhere. There is a nice example at Sheriff Hutton with contemporary rails and York St Cuthbert has a seventeenth-century communion table.

There is a mid-eighteenth-century communion table in the retrochoir at Hull, described by Pevsner as 'a delightful piece'. Another eighteenth-century table is preserved in the north aisle at Wharram-le-Street and there is a pleasant example at Kirkleatham whose carved frontal displays putto heads in spandrels. The communion table in the church at Well possesses an eighteenth-century frontal. (More commonly, the front of the altar is hidden by a rich 'frontal' in textiles with the top edge overhung by a 'super-frontal'.)

Eighteenth-century communion tables (in richer churches at least) were often dignified by a reredos designed in the contemporary taste. There are several good examples of this period in York (then a centre of fashion for the north of England): St Michael-le-Belfrey (1712), Holy Trinity Goodramgate (1721) and the later St Michael Spurriergate and St Martin-cum-Gregory. Hull Holy Trinity has a magnificent table and reredos in the rococo style.

A monumental reredos was designed for Newcastle St Nicholas in *c.* 1700 and this was later dismantled and two sections placed in East Rounton where they are really too grand for the smaller church.

The Anglican revival of the late nineteenth century continued the good work of restoration with a particular emphasis on the return to pre-Reformation styles. Reredoses returned to fashion and some were even imported – for example there is a sixteenth-century Flemish relief at Cayton, the crowded carving from Antwerp (*c.* 1520) at Pocklington and the simpler Dutch work at Well. Beighton has a carved nineteenth-century representation in alabaster of the Last Supper (nineteenth-century Italian) and there is a similar centre-piece to the complex carved wood reredos at Marsden (dating from the early twentieth century).

Alabaster reredoses of a more medieval type were quite frequent and some were painted in a medieval manner, as the one at Burghwallis. The gorgeous piece of carving which provides the reredos at Howden is authentic fifteenth-century work, once part of the pulpitum of the collegiate church.

The popular church architect Street provided a new reredos at Garton-on-the-Wolds (*c.* 1870); that at West Hutton was painted in *c.* 1875. In 1888 Rothwell acquired a reredos in Caen stone with mosaic panels and there is an essay in Art Nouveau at Denaby Main (1899). Temple Moore was responsible for the new altar and reredos at Helmsley (1904?). The altar at Thirsk has been described as 'magnificent' and Patrington commemorated King George V in 1935 by the lavish coloured and gilded reredos of the new high altar (there is a smaller one in the Lady chapel). There is a later printed reredos by Pace and Harvey at Thrybergh, and an exuberant one in carved oak of an earlier date at Bossall. The embroidered triptych of three angels at Guisborough is also from the early twentieth century.

In more tolerant (or understanding) times, recovered altar stones (mensae) were preserved and even restored to something like their original function. Ryther retains five, one of which has been replaced in the sanctuary. Knaresborough has a restored medieval altar in a side chapel. The altar stone preserved at Conisborough is said to come from the castle chapel. One from a minor altar of the former priory is preserved at Bolton Abbey and a medieval mensa exists in the south aisle at Wintringham. Goathland keeps a mensa which allegedly came from a former hermitage in the vicinity. At Nun Monkton the medieval altar stone is inset in the floor under the post-Reformation communion table.

On a different, but related subject, the Anglican church at Campsall safeguards, in the South chapel, a carved and painted stone altar in the Gothic manner by Pugin which was made for the now disused Catholic chapel at Ackworth Grange.

Dignified worship was encouraged by Archbishop Laud who seems to have favoured the covering of the altar table with a rich 'carpet'. This practice is maintained at York St Michael Spurriergate which also retains a late seventeenth-century table-cover in leather.

Having traversed the church from west to east, it remains to look for furniture which may occur in any part of the church. Probably the most interesting group is that of memorials.

MEMORIALS

Memorials may be simply divided into five classes: slabs, brasses, table-tombs with or without effigies, mural tablets and others.

Incised slabs are the simplest survivals and originally served as covers for coffins which were sunk level with the floor. There are many examples (Brodsworth and Lead, for example, where the floor is largely paved with coffin lids) and cannibalized fragments can frequently be found in the church's fabric, especially porches, as at Hampsthwaite and Stanwick.

Some of these stones have been reused to mark later graves in the churchyard (Otley has one and Middleton-on-the-Wolds, four).

In spite of their simplicity, incised slabs represent important burials since only such would have been permitted inside the church. There are two noble Anglo-Saxon examples at Kirkdale, a headstone of c. 1050 at Mirfield, and a late twelfth-century fragment at Birstall. A slab at Butterwick has characteristic Early English ornament as well as a sword and shield. There is a fine thirteenth-century example at Middleton Tyas.

The simplest decoration is usually a cross standing on steps (the so-called Calvary cross). The head of the cross could be elaborated into a flower-like shape (floriated cross), a development of the thirteenth to fourteenth centuries. There are rich examples of such at Nun Monkton, and several at Startforth and Tankesley. The earliest slabs often have, besides the cross, an indication of the profession of the deceased: a chalice for a priest, sword for a knight, or shears for a woolman. (Lastingham has one with cross and chalice, and another with sword; there are two with shears at Forcett, and another at

Bradford.) One of the two slabs at Kilburn has a cross, a round boss and a hammer. There is a fragment with bust and foliated cross at South Cave. Another at Bardsey has a foliated cross and sword. These 'trade marks' are the only clue to the deceased. Most early examples bear no names.

Walkington has an engraved chalice slab to Christopher Watson. Some slabs bear a crozier which indicates not a bishop, but a religious superior (with a possible exception at Kilburn). There is a thirteenth-century example at Oswaldkirk, probably to an abbot of Byland, and another at Brafferton (prior of Newburgh?). A fine incised slab (c. 1260) at Watton commemorates William de Malton, Gilbertine prior. Selby has two worn, but once elaborately detailed, memorial slabs to sixteenth-century abbots. The finely carved tombstone of Robert Thornton, abbot of Jervaulx, is at Middleham.

A floriated cross of 1512 at Pocklington commemorates Margaret Easingwold, once prioress of Wilberfoss. Wycliffe has a fine slab to John Forster, a former rector who died in 1456. Eastrington remembers Thomas de Fortington (†1427) and his wife. Dame Margery is commemorated in a twelfth- to thirteenth-century stone carved with her effigy at Wistow.

Most incised slabs are made from local stone, but there are exceptions. For example, alabaster is used for the slab dated 1461 at Thorpe Salvin.

There are also variations in coffin design: instead of the usual flat lid some were provided with a coped roof and appear to have remained within sight. There is a fine thirteenth-century example at Throapham, a very elaborately carved specimen from the Norman period at Conisborough and a simpler one at Weston.

Other unusual examples might include: the large blue slab at Bowes with a vertical view of a dog at the foot of the cross (fourteenth-century); the double incised mural slab at East Harsley; and the 'serpent stone' (possibly thirteenth-century) at Kellington. The nineteenth-century church at Sproatley preserves a thirteenth-century coffin lid with the usual foliated cross but it also shows a chalice and (uniquely) a hand taking a wafer from a paten. It is inscribed in Norman French: *Ci git Walter Chapelann T . . . kahingham. Priez pour l'ame* ('Here lies Walter, the chaplain T . . . Kehingham [Keyngham?]. Pray for his soul'). There is a remarkable fifteenth-century Pudsey monument at Bolton-by-Bowland consisting of a large marble slab incised with the figures of a husband, three wives and twenty-five children.

Coffin slabs, grave covers or other memorials set flush with the
floor of the church tended to increase in the seventeenth centuries
(for example, the grave cover of 1696 in the floor at Weston). A
characteristic form of the seventeenth to eighteenth centuries was the
'Ledger Stone', a massive slab of marble or blueish-grey stone with a
finely cut inscription in Roman lettering below a heraldic
achievement in bas-relief. Selected examples might include: Beverley
St Mary, Hull Holy Trinity, Grinton, Kirkleatham, Sancton, and York
St Martin-cum-Gregory. Occasionally, ledger-stones were imitated in
cast-iron, as at Sandal Magna.

There are about a hundred brasses in Yorkshire, of varying quality
but few are remarkable. Only the indent remains of what was
probably the finest, that to Robert Rogers, last abbot of Selby
(†1559), at Snaith.

The oldest surviving brass (c. 1360) is the military one at
Aldborough. The North Riding also has a good clerical one (†1550)
at Sessay and a fine civilian one (†1391) at Topcliffe (one of the best
in England) as well as the impressive memorial to the priest Simon de
Wensley (c. 1360) at Wensley. There are three commemorating the
Burgh family at Catterick (dating from the fifteenth century) and
other examples at Bossall (1454 – only partly preserved), Cowthorpe
(1494 – fragmented), Helmsley (c. 1465 – much rubbed), Hornby
(1443 – fragments), Roxby (1523 – poor), Thirsk (1419 – demi) and
Wath (two from the fifteenth century and a third from the sixteenth).
A demi (brass) shows only the upper part of the figure, above the
waist.

Brasses in the East Riding are more numerous and include
examples at Aldbrough (Richard Aske and wife – †1460, probably
from Ellerton priory); Bainton (Roger Godeale, priest – 1429, worn);
Beeford (Thos. Tonge, priest †1472); Bishop Burton (chalice brass
†1460), Ellerker (husband and wife †1521); Brandesburton (remains
of bracket brass to priest †1364); Harpham (large St Quintin husband
and wife †1397); Cottingham (magnificent clerical †1383, civilian
and wife 1504 – on the wall); Flamborough (Marmaduke Constable
c. 1520 – with quaint rhyming inscription); Heslerton (early fifteenth-
century knight); Hull St Mary Lowgate (incised c. 1525); Routh
(couple under canopy, c. 1420); Wilberfoss (small memorial to Robt.
Hoton and wife – 1477); Winestead (husband and wife, c. 1540 –
mutilated); York St Michael Spurriergate (chalice brass to Wm.
Langton 1466).

Of the few in the West Riding the following might be mentioned: Burghwallis (Thomas Gascoigne, kt., †1556); Kirkby Wharfe (William Gisborne, priest, *c.* 1480); Hampsthwaite (civilian, *c.* 1480 – on wall, mutilated); Owston (Thomas de Hatfield and wife, †1409); Ripley (chalice brass, 1429); Sprotborough (William fitzWilliam and wife †1474 – fine).

There are a number of matrices (the indents of lost brasses) at Beverley and Ellerton.

The practice of providing brass memorial tablets (of decreasing sophistication) continued after the Reformation. The church at Rotherham has a table commemorating a civilian and his wife (1561) and Kilnwick Percy a brass of 1584. The example at Otley (1593) bears a genealogical tree of the Lyndley and Palmer families.

There are seventeenth-century brasses at Bradfield, Burnby, Kirby Malzeard and Rawmarsh. One at Welwick commemorates William Wright of Ploughland (†1621), 'elder brother of two Gunpowder plotters'. York All Saints North St. has a 1642 brass commemorating a tanner. Another at Birstall bears a figure of Mrs Popeley in her shroud (1623). There is an unusually good brass of 1631+ at Kirkleatham. An example from the eighteenth century at Middleton Tyas tells of the Revd John Mawer (†1763) who was 'descended from king Coyl' and knew twenty-two languages. Somewhat lesser folk had small inscribed brass plates fixed to their headstones in the churchyard. Some 200 of these are preserved inside the parish church of Scarborough.

EFFIGIES

Characteristically, effigies are found recumbent in a wall niche or on a table-tomb but it has been pointed out that, after the Reformation, they increasingly adopt a more upright and proud position.

Though later Tudor injunctions expressly excluded images of the secular great from the general iconoclasm of the Reformation, they were too late to save some, and others subsequently suffered the ravages of the Puritans and more recent vandals. There has also been neglect and wear which has left hardly a trace of the original bright colours with which the monuments were once painted and gilded.

Medieval knights are sometimes portrayed in a cross-legged position. This was once taken to mean that they had been Crusaders but, in fact, this attitude is merely an early fourteenth-century fashion in monumental sculpture. (There are early fourteenth-century knightly effigies with straight legs at, for example, Ingleby Arncliffe, Melsonby and, conversely, there is a cross-legged civilian at Stonegrave.)

Men often rest their head on a helm and their feet on a lion; women usually have a cushion at their head and a dog at their feet but exceptions are worth looking for.

Effigies are normally carved in oak, stone or alabaster. There are Savile monuments in both oak and alabaster at Thornhill. Examples in oak rarely survive because of decay. (At Swillington fragments of an oak effigy have been sealed in a glass case within an ogee recess in the south aisle. There are several badly worm-eaten figures of the fourteenth century at Allerton Mauleverer.)

The finest Yorkshire oaken effigy is at Barnbrough: the monument to Sir Thomas Cresacre who died in 1348, allegedly as the result of a fight with a wild cat in the church porch. The monument is executed with both skill and sensitivity. There is another fine figure, roughly contemporary, at Whorlton-in-Cleveland. At Worsborough the rare 'double-decker' timber monument to Roger Rockley (†1534) has a cadaver in the lower 'bunk' and a crudely-painted effigy of the deceased in the upper.

Effigies in stone or alabaster are too numerous to list: in the North Riding alone they occur in some 40 churches (of which West Tanfield has 7; Bedale and Hornby 5; Stanwick 4; Acklam, South Cowton and Pickering 3 each). (One of the two at Sheriff Hutton commemorates the only son of Richard II.) The fourteenth-century Fitzalan monument at Bedale portrays Sir Brian in alabaster and his wife in stone.

Stone effigies tend to be earlier than alabaster and are often placed in wall recesses, often with an ogee arch above, as at Goldsborough, Knaresborough, Ilkley, Thornton Steward and Wath. A recess in the north wall at Birkin holds an early fourteenth-century effigy of a cross-legged civilian (as at Stonegrave). He holds his heart in his hand and his draperies exhibit bold, unconventional carving.

Filey has an unusual thirteenth-century miniature effigy of a priest which probably represents a heart burial. There is a late thirteenth-century knight at Pickhill, and a knight and his lady in a cusped recess at Felixkirk (c. 1300). The effigy of Sir Hugh FitzHenry at Romaldkirk is dated 1304 and Kirby Fleetham has an excellent early fourteenth-century knight. There is an equally good lady with angels by her pillow at Kirby Sigston. Slingsby has an early fourteenth-century knight and there is a fine lady, with her head under a canopy, of the same period at Thornton-le-Dale. At South Anston there is a (unique?) monument with effigies of a lady and her daughter.

There is a particularly fine knight (*c.* 1320–30) at East Harsley: bare-headed, clothed in chain mail and a dramatically draped mantle. Two knights of *c.* 1330 at Ingleby Arncliffe have their hearts in their hands and provide interest for the student of armour in their 'ailettes' (compare with those at Wilton, near Whitby).

Crathorne has an early fourteenth-century knight in the cross-legged posture of the period. There is also a unique, but unfortunately almost unrecognizable effigy of a deacon. The monuments to a priest and a knight at Ingleby Greenhow are also very disfigured. Stainton has a fourteenth-century effigy of a civilian and Catterick has a later fourteenth-century knight without a sword (similar to the example at Kirklington). There is a fine fourteenth-century priest at Thwing, although two others at Thryburgh are sadly defaced.

The effigy of Sir John de Sutton (†1357) at Sutton (Humberside) rests on a splendid alabaster tomb-chest, of which there are many others (at Harewood, Methley, Swine, Tickhill and Thornhill, for example). Wadworth has an unusual representation of a knight in hunting garb (he was Forester of Hatfield Chace). Pickering has three knights: two from the mid-fourteenth century, and one from *c.* 1400. There is a vested priest, holding a chalice, in the fifteenth-century monument at Great Langton.

One of the earliest alabaster effigies in England occurs at Bedale: the animated carving of an early fourteenth-century knight. There is a later one (+1446) at Barmston on a tomb-chest with angels holding shields (a common device in the Perpendicular period).

Some tomb-chests did not carry effigies. The most famous example is perhaps the Brus cenotaph (Guisborough) but there are less elaborate examples such as the Vavasour tombs at Weston. One of these, dating from the thirteenth century, has a pitched roof and the ornament is confined to sword, shield and the family arms. The other (1587+) is severe and only bears heraldry (recently restored).

Some monuments fall between effigies and slabs. They consist of rectangular flat stones with the upper and lower portions hollowed out and filled with representations of head and feet as though the deceased was under a very short cover. There are examples at Gilling, Goodmanham, Moor Monkton and Wadworth. A ninth-century

Anglo-Saxon sculpture at Otley shows what is perhaps a precedent for this curious design.

The strange monument at Lowthorpe, however, seems without precedent. It probably commemorates Sir Thos. Heslerton who founded a chantry in the church in 1364. The memorial portrays a couple in early fourteenth-century costume lying side by side and covered by a sheet. This in turn is overlaid by a tree whose branches terminate in the heads of thirteen children. At the root of the tree are heraldic shields. The concept is a kind of secular version of the Tree of Jesse.

Renaissance influences were slow to take effect. North Cave has two recumbent effigies in alabaster of *c.* 1600 (compare with the example dated 1602 at Winestead). The tomb-chest has disappeared. An Elizabethan version of the chest without the figures occurs at Hornby (1578), and there are characteristic effigies at Kirklington (+1590), Well (+1596), Coxwold (1603) and Masham (+1613) where the figure begins to rise on its elbow. It is on its knees at Richmond St Mary (1629), Nether Poppleton (1620) and Wentworth (1614) and standing in the Spilsby monuments at Knaresborough (Sir Henry in his shroud; Sir William in outdoor costume: both dated 1634).

Easington has a monument to a baby (†1621) complete with cradle and bedclothes.

A new type of monument appears in the slab supported only at the corners (Cumberland (1632)). At Londesborough it is supported on four marble jars, a design which is repeated at Roxby for Lady Boynton (1634). There are four marble putti in the Nevile monument (1673) at Royston.

The frontal demi-figure appears in the seventeenth century; there are examples at Cawood (1651), Kirk Deighton (1656), Skirpenbeck (1636). There is a recoloured example, and bust, at Nether Poppleton (1651), and two in York St Martin Coney St. dated 1633 and 1636. But there are still recumbent effigies (Knaresborough, 1602; Wighill, +1634; Langton, 1656 (recoloured); Lockington, *c.* 1630; Kirkheaton, +1631), though some have adopted the sideways position (Ecclesfield 1640).

Classical design is first displayed in the Harrison monument (†1656) with no figures (Leeds St John Briggate), but the older forms persist: the Bolles (†1662) are recumbent at Ledsham, as are Wentworth and his wife (1665+) at Wentworth, (two others of *c.* 1685 are kneeling).

The confidence and elegance characteristic of the eighteenth century start to show in the later seventeenth century (Sherburnes at Great Mitton (*c.* 1690), and Lewises at Ledsham (1677), for example) and are established in the Irwin monument at Whitkirk (first decade of the eighteenth century) and in the Pilkington memorial at Wakefield (†1714).

The names of famous sculptors begin to appear in this period: a tablet by Rysbrack at South Kirkby (1720), and the purely architectural monument at Nunnington (1743); busts by Guelfi at Kirkthorpe and Kirkheaton (1731); work by Scheemakers at Barnby Dun (1733), Ledsham (1739), Methley (1741) and Bradford (1742).

There is good work by unknown or lesser-known artists at Darton (1722), Long Marston (1740), Adlingfleet (1745), Burton Agnes (1759), Coxwold (1700) and Harpham (1762).

Later work includes that of Nollekens at Whitkirk (1810), and Flaxman at Bradford (1796), Campsall (1803), Wragby (1806), Rotherham (1806), Wortley (1808), and Leeds parish church (1811). The Yorkshire sculptor Chantrey produced monuments at Sheffield (1805), and others at Wragby, Owston and Snaith (1837). Other notable examples might include anonymous work at Kirk Ella of 1809 and the Edwardian monuments at Warter.

An artificial stone was invented by Coade in the late eighteenth century and was used for monuments at Aston in 1797 and Kirkby Overblow in 1793.

The sepulchral conceits that began with shrouds in the seventeenth century and included skulls, Father Time, etc., developed into allegorical or symbolic figures, the latter exemplified by the figure of the elder Fauconberg in Roman garb (†1700) on a memorial at Coxwold. Perhaps this genre reaches its apogee in the surgeon's monument at Bradford (1833) of which the chief feature is a free-standing half-naked Greek maiden.

The seventeenth-century 'shroud' had its antecedents in the medieval 'cadaver' which portrayed a decaying body (as at Hemingborough) and reappears in the seventeenth century (as at Bishop Burton).

WALL TABLETS

Some of the memorials already mentioned could be described as elaborate three-dimensional wall tablets. A noteworthy eighteenth-century example at Goldsborough is based on a classical reredos, ornamented with medallions depicting members of the Byerley family. Against this background stand life-size figures of Faith and Charity, assisted by two putti, attending to an urn.

The wall tablet proper is, of course, much simpler though it can be elaborated to a greater or lesser extent.

Its interest is perhaps mainly for the genealogist or the local historian. The set at Otley, for example, dates from the early seventeenth to mid-nineteenth centuries and records several local families. It also shows a wide variety of design: rectangular tablets with square pediments, niches flanked by balusters, a variety of strap-work decoration, added brass plates, reliefs and portrait medallions, heraldry, lettering of different styles and inscriptions that vary both in length and nature.

The following list details what the explorer might look for:

a) a memorial of general interest. Little Driffield, for example, has a tablet recording that the church is on the site of the burial place of Alfrith, a king of Northumbria who died of his wounds in 705 after a battle with the Danes;

b) extra-parochial significance of the person commemorated (Sydney Smith at Foston, for instance);

c) good lettering and design (as on Wormley tablet at Foston);

d) memorials to 'old, unhappy, far-off things and battles long ago', (Stafford at Wentworth, Gully at Ackworth, Bishop Wilson at Askrigg, Flodden memorial at Arncliffe, nineteen-year-old victim of 'Dotheboys Hall' (Bowes), Royalist incumbent persecuted by Parliamentarians (Birkin);

e) epitaphs: simple, orotund, pathetic, amusing. No examples will be given as the interested will prefer to make their own collection, but compare those of John Bright (Badsworth), Thomas Jackson (Nunnington), Mary Ward (Osbaldwick), Robert Lyth (Snainton);

f) curiosities: for example, the female churchwarden (1667) at Appleton Wiske, 169-year-old Jenkins (Bolton-on-Swale), 31 in tall Ridesdale (Hampsthwaite).

Another form of memorial is the funeral hatchment: armorial shields painted on wood or canvas and set in a lozenge-shaped frame. They were displayed at the home of the deceased, carried in the funeral cortege and then 'laid up' in the local church. Hatchments used to be found quite commonly in churches, particularly in those close to a great house. They are now becoming rare but occasionally survive, as at Downholme, Easby, Hemingborough and Weston. There is a very rare funeral banner at Londesborough and other banners at Kirby Underdale.

INSCRIPTIONS

Many of the best medieval memorials took the form of building a church, or adding to the furnishings of an existing one. Bishop Skirlaugh provided an entire church for his native village as did some Anglo-Saxon nobility (consider also the dedication stone at York St Mary Castlegate).

This generosity was marked by inscriptions or the equivalent armorial identification. Many of the latter are indecipherable through wear or the loss of blazoning and most of the former are lost. (They normally took the form of an 'Orate' – a request for prayer – or an assumption that the pious would remember them in their orisons.)

Inscriptions occur on the Anglo-Saxon sundials at Great Edstone, Kirkdale and the Norman dial at Weaverthorpe.

They also appear on fonts at Bingley (Runes), Goodmanham, South Kilvington and the equivalent armorial memento on many Perpendicular examples (for example, Catterick).

The record may be indirect (the westernmost north window at Ecclesfield, for example, refers to Coventry Charterhouse who provided both it and the chancel) or it may consist only of initials or a rebus (stalls at Wensley and screens at Owston and Hubberholme).

The Cresacre arms are (just) decipherable on the tower at Barnburgh and there are inscriptions on the towers of Barwick-in-Elmet, Bolton Abbey and Thornton-in-Craven.

Those in the nave at Beverley St Mary include the delightful memorial of the minstrels' contribution to the rebuilding. There is an inscription on a pier at Carnaby and on the porch at South Cowton. Others occur on a bench at Ecclesfield, the roof at Darton, a door at Worsborough and the head of the churchyard cross at Pocklington.

In the later Middle Ages, windows were a frequent result of individual or corporate generosity and usually recorded the fact. There are examples in York All Saints North St. and an interesting collection in the Savile chapel at Thornhill, of which one was the gift of the parson.

This practice survived the Reformation. There is an inscribed Jacobean pulpit at Huntingdon and there are many more recent examples recorded at the foot of stained glass windows or on unobtrusive brass plates affixed to various items of church furniture.

MISCELLANEA

Apart from the upper storey of a porch, a church may have provided accommodation elsewhere – in the tower perhaps or over some vestries. Chambers are built into the upper structure of the nave at Campsall, Wadworth and Yarm. Above the North chapel and sacristy at Beverley is the so-called 'priest's room', a considerable chamber now housing a dusty collection of ecclesiastical 'bygones'. It is approached by a most ingenious spiral stair which ends under a charming vault.

Already mentioned are anchorites, recluses confined to their cell which frequently was attached to a church. Literary records exist of such cells at Ainderby, Kexby (church replaced in 1852), Layton (replaced 1895), Ravenser (lost to erosion), Thorganby, and half a dozen in York. (The one at All Saints North St. was reconstructed in the early twentieth century (in concrete and half-timber!) but currently lacks an inmate.) Tenuous indications of a former anchorage may be found in some churches, Conisborough, Grinton, Kirkburton, Riccall and Skipton, for instance.

The sanctuary area of a church often contains a splendid chair, for the benefit of a visiting bishop. These are worth looking for, and there are examples at Bolton-by-Bowland, Darrington, Harpham, Hemingborough, Hubberholme and Selby. Some of the more ancient chairs are made of stone and called 'Frith stools'. They are said to have conferred sanctuary on fugitives who grasped them (there are examples at Beverley Minster and possibly Sprotborough and Halsham).

Chandeliers are an attractive Georgian contribution to church furnishing. There are good examples at Bishop Wilton, Giggleswick, Helmsley, Pickering, Scrayingham, Slaidburn, Wath-on-Dearne, Whitby, Winestead, Wycliffe, York St Martin-cum-Gregory. Other instances include Rokeby (domestic), Brompton (immense Victorian) and Owston (modern).

Parish churches had at least one strong-box or chest for safe-keeping their possessions. They are usually provided with three different locks so that they could only be opened by incumbent and churchwardens together. They vary greatly in design and sophistication, from 'dug-outs' to fine examples of the carpenter's art. Crayke has two 'dug-outs', Salton-in-Ryedale an early thirteenth-century piece, Kirkleatham and Wath-on-Dearne have magnificent fourteenth-century chests, Hatfield has two (possibly from the sixteenth century and there are well-carved early sixteenth-century examples at Gilling and North Frodingham. In some cases (Hampsthwaite for instance) aesthetics are completely sacrificed for the sake of security.

I give the name 'construct' to an item cannibalizing material which originally belonged to some other furnishing. The font at Hauxwell, stall-backs at Hayton, the reading-desk at Hemingborough, screens at Mitton and Winestead, and the pulpit at Kirklington are all created from this 'cannibalized' material.

A cresset stone is a flat stone furnished with saucer-like depressions which once held oil or fat to fuel primitive lighting. There are survivals at Burnsall, Collingham and Westow. The latter has twelve 'lights' and, mysteriously, has a carved twelfth-century crucifix underneath.

Anglo-Saxon crosses are often the oldest indication of a church's existence. There are scores of fragments in Yorkshire churches (with notable examples at, for example, Middleton). They are often associated with hog-backs – a recumbent tombstone with a sloping upper surface and ornamented on sides and ends (see the collection at Brompton-in-Allertonshire). The interested explorer might pursue the subject in W.G. Collingwood's *Northumbrian Crosses of the pre-Norman Age* (now in paperback).

Decoration takes many forms. In the Middle Ages colour was applied to every possible surface: fonts, screens, pulpits, tombs, statuary, walls (see murals below), roof bosses and other architectural details (for example, at Easby, Hessle and South Cave). In the later medieval period, the blazonry of heraldry (see below) was everywhere. Apart from murals, there was figure painting on wooden panels of reredoses, dadoes of screens, even ceilings. The whole interior would have been lit by multi-coloured, but far from dim, light which filtered through the stained glass windows.

Chancels were sometimes floored with encaustic tiles (tiles inlaid with differently coloured clays burnt in) but, generally speaking, medieval floor material seems to have been rather primitive. There is a magnificent nineteenth-century chancel floor in mosaic at Hornby, a good design in the nineteenth-century tiled chancel at Alne, a beautifully tiled floor at Great Mitton, interesting use of red brick at Stillington and good early twentieth-century flooring at Bishop Wilton.

Occasionally churches preserve pieces of funeral armour which once formed part of the complete array of aristocratic funeral effects. Rare pieces survive at Marr, Methley and Stanwick.

Heraldry: the right to bear arms was *the* status symbol of the Middle Ages, eagerly sought and jealously guarded. It was so pervasive that even Christ, His mother and the saints were provided with 'arms' (the Five Wounds, fleur-de-lys, gridiron, etc.). The carving of donors' arms on church furniture was an effective way of commemorating the benefactor and is frequently found in the Perpendicular period. There are shields on the towers of Aughton, Croft, Hatfield, Methley, Ripley and Wintringham; on many fonts of the fourteenth century and later (for example at Beverley St Mary, Catterick, Goodmanham and Mappleton), and often only heraldic symbols survive from the glass of a medieval window (as at Ellerton, Hull St Mary, Kilham, Kirby Wharfe, Leconfield, Newton Kyme, Thorpe Basset and Thirsk). The Percy badge appears on the piers at Leathley, on the rood-screen at Hubberholme and on stalls at Wakefield (which also bear the Savile arms). The Boynton arms appear on the south front of the chancel at South Cowton, and those of Scrope within the chancel-arch at Wensley, and there are armorials on the fabric of Grinton. Noble tombs are a natural location for heraldry (Beverley, Bubwith, Methley and Skipton) as are family chapels (Lockington, Sprotborough, Thornhill and Wensley). Secular heraldry survived the Reformation. There is restrained eighteenth-century work on the fabric at Patrick Brompton, heraldic ceilings to the nave and chancel at Halifax (1636) and seventeenth-century heraldic glass at Goldsborough and Roos. Eighteenth-century armorial glass exists at Coxwold, Harpham, Thornhill and Weston and there are some Georgian shields at Thwing and much twentieth-century work at Kirk Bramwith. Ledger stones bear heraldic arms within a circular depression.

Metalwork is worth looking for. It may be the work of the village blacksmith (like the chancel-gates at Burghwallis, window fittings at Hubberholme and the communion rail at Boynton) or more sophisticated work such as the great screen at Bishop Wilton or the recycled gates at Bawtry and Harthill. There is a fine seventeenth-century bracket for the font cover at Knaresborough, a good eighteenth-century gate in the south porch at Wakefield and an elegant nineteenth-century screen round a tomb at Kirkleatham. There is eighteenth-century ironwork supporting a communion table at Beverley and a good nineteenth-century brass screen at Fimber.

Mosaics are not common in English church decoration. There are good mosaic floors at Bishop Wilton, Garton-on-the-Wolds and Hornby. At Kirkby Grindalythe the whole west wall is covered by a mosaic representing the Ascension. The best work, however, is at St Aidan's, Leeds, where there are mosaics by Sir Frank Brangwyn in the apse and round the quire.

The most extensive survivals of medieval murals are at Easby, dating from the mid-thirteenth century, and Pickering, from the fifteenth, but there are fragmentary remains in many places (Bedale, Kirby Hill (Boroughbridge), Marr, Romaldkirk, Royston, South Cowton and Wensley). Thirsk has faded seventeenth-century paintings of apostles on clerestory walls and Father Time appears (just) at Spennithorpe. There are nineteenth-century angels at Bolton-on-Swale and a decorated east wall and roof at Bolton Abbey. The most remarkable example of post-Reformation mural painting, however, is the complete scheme of 1872–80 at Garton-on-the-Wolds, recently restored as a fitting memorial to N. Pevsner.

Some churches retain musical instruments from the days before the Victorian organ became general. There are, for example, barrel-organs at Holme-on-Spalding-Moor (allegedly from the seventeenth century), Skelton near Guisborough (eighteenth century), and Farnham (1831). Hutton Rudby has a bassoon, there is a pitch-pipe at Whorlton and vamping horns at Whitby. A pair of ophicleides is preserved at nearby Lythe. The organ itself, a common feature, has an organ case which sometimes displays fine woodwork. Wakefield has a splendid example given in 1743 and those at Thornton and Wragby date from the early Georgian period. The fine eighteenth-century case at Rotherham holds an early (Snetzler) organ. Occasionally, the case has received highly decorative painting. There is a superb example by Bodley (1862) at Scarborough St Martin and another by J. Oldrid Scott at Halifax. Decorative work by Temple Moore appears at Old Malton (1888) and Brompton, North Riding (1893), an example by Comper (1937) at Frickley and work by G. Pace at Pocklington (1954), York Holy Trinity Micklegate (1964) and Penistone (1976). Pevsner describes the early twentieth-century painting at Tadcaster as 'a work of almost Chinese delicacy and refinement'.

As far as painting is concerned, in medieval times colour was applied to architectural features like the soffits of arches (at Easby and Marr). The mouldings of doors (Whixley) and bosses (whether wood or stone) were also coloured and gilded. There are traces on the chancel arch at South Cowton and the arcade capitals at Hessle still show the remains of painted scrolls.

There is a tendency to emphasise mural paintings, but painting on wooden panels, reredoses, the dadoes of screens, and even ceilings was common (special attention was given to the decoration of the ceiling above the Great Rood and over the high altar (compare the modern equivalent at Bugthorpe). Sutton (Humberside) has a painted panel of St James which was probably the back-plate of a post-Reformation pulpit.

No medieval 'easel' paintings have survived in Yorkshire but there are later ones at Allerton Mauleverer and Masham and the Anglican revival of the later nineteenth-century saw painting being brought in from abroad (for example, the imitation Corregio at Lastingham, the Italian painting (c. 1500) of the Resurrection at Hickleton and the Flemish 'Adoration' at Upper Poppleton).

The Reformers preferred the written word to pictures and (in addition to the Ten Commandments), they painted Biblical texts on the church walls (there is an eighteenth-century example in arch-spandrels at Dunholme). The south wall of the chancel at North Cave is uniquely painted with the Rubrick for Confession and Absolution.

Several churches have unremarkable plasterwork on their ceilings (a fashion introduced in the eighteenth century) but there is superb work on the east wall at Sowerby and Tong (Bradford) has pretty decoration on the chancel ceiling. Boynton has a Gothick plaster vault to the tower and there is eighteenth-century work at Coxwold, on the east wall of the nave, and at Romaldkirk, on the chancel roof. There is some evidence that external walls were plastered in the Middle Ages and then lime-washed. Internal walls were generally plastered to provide a surface for mural paintings.

The Poor Box seems to have been a post-Reformation item of church furniture though there is an alleged medieval example at Speeton. The nicely-decorated box at Knaresborough is dated 1600 and there are Jacobean examples at Bedale, Kirkthorpe and Skipwith (1615). Dated examples exist at Sedbergh (1633), Giggleswick (1684), and the famous 'Old Tristram' at Halifax (dated 1701 – which is almost certainly too late!). Others exist at Scalby (possibly from the seventeenth century), Wintringham (seventeenth century) and York St Martin-cum-Gregory.

Since it was the most substantial building in the neighbourhood, a church tower was sometimes designed to provide a refuge against natural disaster or human hostility. The capacious tower at Drax is said to have been built to accommodate refugees from frequent local flooding. The tower at Bedale was defensive with its battlemented top and entrance guarded by a portcullis, while the stone-vaulted and battlemented two-storeyed porch at Kirkby Moorside is not unlike one of the pele-towers (defensive towers against the Scots) of the area. The constricted doorway into the tower from the nave at Long Preston is overhung by a sort of machicolation.

Both the structure and decoration of roofs and ceilings are worth examining. Apart from the unique painted ceiling at Beverley St Mary, the following are notable examples: Almondbury, Bolton Percy, Burton Agnes, Cawood (the North chapel), Drax, Ecclesfield, Goodmanham, Great Mitton, Hatfield (the North and South chapels), Hull, Kirk Bramwith, Leeds St John, Methley (aisle), Nafferton, Rotherham, South Kirby (north aisle), Wakefield and York All Saints North St.

The explorer might care to collect his own favourite examples of towers and spires. The following are offered as 'starters': Beverley St Mary, Coxwold, Driffield, Hedon, Hemingborough, Howden, Hull, Kirby Hill (Ravensworth), Northallerton, Ottringham, Patrington, Rotherham, Thirsk, Tickhill, Wakefield, Weaverthorpe, Womersley and York St Mary Castlegate.

Wells and springs were regarded as sacred in pre-Christian times and Christian missionaries may well have taken them over by associating them with saints such as Chad or Helen. Some doubtless had acquired a Christian aura by being used in baptism and thus 'holy wells' may be found in association with a church. Some writers have dubiously seen the title of the churches at Middleham and Giggleswick (Alkelda) as being a corruption of a hybrid word meaning 'holy well'. (In 1890 two 'holy wells' were recorded at Giggleswick: one near the railway station, the other in a field near the school. Neither seems to have born the name of Alkelda and their association was with the cleansing of money in time of plague.)

Occasionally springs or wells may be found in churchyards. There is a delightful example at Hinderwell ('St Hilda's well'), North Yorkshire. There are also rare examples of wells inside the church building (for example, at Beverley Minster).

CURIOSITIES

The contents of a church may include many curious items, with equally curious reasons as to why they are there. Or perhaps there will be curiosities for which there are no plausible explanations. These curiosities may include almost anything from a bier to a barrel-organ, a constable's truncheon to a chained book, the parish coffin to a plough or a mace-rest to a miner's lamp. There may be hat-pegs on the wall or a silver trowel in a glass case. There are Roman relics and runic inscriptions, cast-iron fonts and brass chandeliers. There are sloping or undulating floors, 'drunken' fonts and leaning towers. There are doors that lead nowhere and windows that admit no light.

Imagery can be particularly curious: there are pilgrim rabbits and fighting centaurs, cats and fiddles and many strange beasts. The churchyard may have memorials representing a church organ, a railway-tunnel or even the pyramid of Gizeh.

THE TOP TEN

One is frequently asked to identify the 'best' churches and this is an invidious task since selection depends so much on personal taste and interest. I have selected my own favourite ten churches from each of the old Ridings.

East Riding	North Riding	West Riding
Beverley St Mary	Alne	Adel
Hedon	Coxwold	Arksey
Flamborough	Easby	Birkin
Hemingborough	Kirkdale	Bolton Percy
Holme-on-	Lastingham	Burghwallis
Spalding-Moor	Pickering	Fishlake
Hull Holy Trinity	Thirsk	Halifax
North Newbald	Wensley	Hatfield
Patrington	West Tanfield	Sprotborough
York:	Whitby	Tickhill
All Saints		
North Street		
Holy Trinity		
Goodramgate		

Reserves: Ecclesfield, Kirk Hammerton

I would like to conclude with the words of the late Alec Clifton-Taylor, a discerning lover of English buildings:

> England's largest county has memorable churches of almost every type and period. The finest area is scenically the least spectacular, the East Riding, which contains some magnificent church architecture.
>
> The West Riding, in addition to many sandstone churches which in the industrial regions have turned nearly black, can show notable white magnesium limestone buildings in its south-eastern area and rough but likable structures in the Pennines.
>
> The North Riding has no churches of special distinction but a number that are well worth visiting, and in their settings the North Riding churches are the most fortunate of the three.
>
> It should not be forgotten that considerable parts of Yorkshire are still sparsely populated and have never needed more than small and widely scattered places of worship; whereas, on the other hand, the churches of the industrial districts, as in Lancashire, are mostly Victorian. The distribution of notable churches in Yorkshire is therefore very uneven.

It is true that notable churches in Yorkshire are unevenly distributed, but churches of interest can be found throughout the county and, to my mind, there are none which do not offer something to the receptive visitor.

GAZETTEER

The Gazetteer contains a list, in alphabetical order, many of the parish churches of the historic county. It is not complete, specifically it is limited to Anglican churches, but it contains all medieval churches and many others of interest.

In each entry the heading is followed by an abbreviation, first of the old Riding then of the modern 'county'. This is to enable the reader to make use of old guides (such as the invaluable Pevsner, Methuen's 'Little Guides' etc.) as well as later works. The modern divisions are North Yorkshire, Cleveland, West Yorkshire and Humberside. Under the modern reorganization, some parts of ancient Yorkshire have been lost to County Durham, Cumbria and Lancashire. Such examples are indicated in the entry.

Finally, there is a map reference, consisting of two letters and four numbers, giving the positions of all places shown on the quarter-inch Ordnance Survey Map in terms of the National Grid. The letters indicate the appropriate 100 km square. The first two numbers indicate the number of kilometres east from the south-west corner of the appropriate square, the second two similarly indicate the distance in kilometres north from that corner.

NOTES AND ABBREVIATIONS

The following abbreviations are used in the Gazetteer. Where dates are given they are an approximate indication only.

Medieval – *c.* 500–*c.*1500
A/S – Anglo-Saxon: *c.* 600–*c.* 1066
A/D – Anglo-Danish: *c.* 800–*c.* 1066
Norman – *c.* 1066–*c.* 1150
Trans. – Transitional: *c.* 1150–*c.* 1200
EE – Early English: roughly thirteenth century
Dec. – Decorated: *c.* 1300–*c.* 1350
Perp. – Perpendicular: *c.* 1350–*c.* 1550
Eliz. – Elizabethan: *c.* 1550–*c.* 1600
Jacobean – *c.* 1600–1640

Later seventeenth century – *c.* 1660–1700
Georgian – 1714–*c.* 1830
Victorian – 1830–1900

ER East Riding
NR North Riding
WR West Riding

C Cumbria
Cl Cleveland
D County Durham
H Humberside
L Lancashire
NY North Yorkshire
SY South Yorkshire
WY West Yorkshire

R Redundant. Where this abbreviation follows the name of the church it indicates that the church is no longer in regular use.

ADDINGHAM   ST PETER   WR (WY) SE 0749

Built *c.* 1475 (the original nave roof survives) when a member of the local Vavasour family unusually held the position of both squire and rector. Much altered in 1757 and chancel restored in 1875. Interesting fragment of late A/S cross. Eighteenth-century font. Cutting of Glastonbury thorn said to be in churchyard.

ADEL   ST JOHN BAPTIST   WR (WY) SE 3135

Perhaps finest Norman church in county. Undeveloped two-cell plan with nineteenth-century bell-cote which probably resembles original. Magnificent south portal and door retains rare Norman ring of excellent quality. Fine external decoration with elaborately carved corbel-table. Magnificent chancel-arch with carving of baptism and crucifixion of Christ among other subjects.

ADLINGFLEET   ALL SAINTS   WR (H) SE 8421

Essentially of the thirteenth century with late twelfth-century doorway and fifteenth-century tower. The porch has fifteenth-century panels of Annunciation, Coronation and Assumption of the Blessed Virgin Mary. Monuments of fourteenth, sixteenth and urbane eighteenth century.

ADWICK-LE-STREET ST LAURENCE   WR (SY) SE 5308
Norman doorway, EE north chapel and sedilia. Perp. north aisle and
windows. Tomb-chests and sixteenth-century slab with Washington
arms, said to have inspired US flag. East window of north chapel has
1940s glass depicting life of St Francis of Assisi.

ADWICK-UPON-DEARNE ST JOHN   WR (SY) SE 4601
Simple Norman two-celled church, now pebble-dashed. Rare
retention of original bell-cote. EE windows and possibly chancel-arch.

AINDERBY STEEPLE ST HELEN   NR (NY) SE 3392
Name indicates that 'steeple' means imposing tower, not necessarily
with a spire. The tower (never designed for a spire) is Perp. but the
body of the church is of earlier Dec. period (compare the piscina,
sedilia, canopied niches). Clerestory and south porch are Perp. Font is
dated 1662. Lectern of *c*. 1900.

ALDBOROUGH ST ANDREW   WR (NY) NZ 2011
Nave and aisle *c*. 1360, Perp. clerestory, chancel and squat tower
which provide a characteristic silhouette. South aisle rebuilt 1827.
Panelled nave roof with bosses (Perp.). Seventeenth-century pulpit
with inscription, communion rails *c*. 1700, rare eighteenth-century
bread shelves. Roman altar from Isurium Brigantium, whose site is
partly occupied by church. Large brass of *c*. 1360 attached to north
wall of nave. Bits of fourteenth-century glass and windows by Kempe.

ALDBROUGH ST BARTHOLOMEW   ER (H) TA 2338
Stands within circular churchyard. Slight Norman remains in chancel
but dates mainly from the thirteenth to fourteenth centuries.
Victorian arcades. Rare A/S sundial inscribed: Ulf who ordered this
church to be built for [the good of] his own and Gunware's souls.
Carving of small Roman soldier at north side of south aisle (date
unknown). Later fourteenth-century tomb-chest with lady under
canopy. Tomb-chest of John de Melsa (Meaux) †1377 with effigy.
Twentieth-century glass in east window.

ALDFIELD ST LAURENCE   NR (NY) SE 2669
Rare eighteenth-century church (*c*. 1783) but dedication suggests it
replaces much earlier building. Small and chapel-like in pleasant

churchyard. Perfectly preserved interior of period: three-decker pulpit, box pews and plastered ceiling.

ALLERSTON   ST MARY   NR (NY) SE 8782
Perp. tower dominates the neighbourhood and the church has a generally Perp. appearance but the chancel is Dec. Recycled Norman material and later coffin slabs built into walls.

ALLERTON MAULEVERER   NR (NY) SE 8782

ST MARTIN (R)

Substantially eighteenth-century church with a Norman appearance. Fourteenth-century arcade. Seventeenth-century hammer-beam roof and contemporary Jacobean pulpit and pews. Font, a little glass in east window, and painting of Moses and Aaron come from the eighteenth century. Early fourteenth-century oak effigies in poor state, rare brass of c. 1400, damaged alabaster effigies (1468+). West front is fascinating example of eighteenth-century 'Gothick' design.

ALMONDBURY   ALL HALLOWS   WR (WY) SE 1614
Big church, largely rebuilt in later fifteenth century but EE chancel survives. Battlements and pinnacles from nineteenth-century restoration. Magnificent nave roof with bosses, etc. (1522). Perp. font cover is one of best in Yorkshire. Two medieval chests, substantial fragments of fifteenth-century glass in North (Kaye) chapel. Family pew (1605). Early Georgian lectern.

ALNE   ST MARY   NR (NY) SE 4965
In spite of appearances, a Norman church almost entirely. The magnificent south doorway, with its unique decoration, is described by Pevsner as 'fully Norman and typically Yorkshire'. The tower was heightened and otherwise modified in eighteenth century. Medieval alterations include Dec. windows and chapel and Perp. north arcade. Fine Norman font, alabaster effigy of the fourteenth century, pulpit of 1626. Also said to have rare survival of Maiden's Garland (a simple wreath carried at young girl's funeral, then hung in church).

AMOTHERBY   ST HELEN   NR (NY) SE 7473
Some original Norman work (including doorway) survives neo-

Norman rebuilding of 1872. Tower of *c.* 1600 (at least in details). Sculptural fragments (A/D, Norman, and remains of thirteenth-century tomb-chest) in porch. Two interesting coffin lids and fine early fourteenth-century effigy.

AMPLEFORTH ST HILDA   NR (NY) SE 5878
Largely rebuilt in 1868, but Norman work survives in north doorway and font, Trans. in south doorway and EE in chancel. Under tower fragmentary remains of very strange monument (*c.* 1330).

APPLETON-LE-STREET ALL SAINTS   NR (NY) SE 7373
A/S tower of tenth century with upper stage of twelfth century. Rest mainly EE. Norman font, fragmentary seated Virgin in niche on tower (of the thirteenth century?), two good effigies of ladies (one *c.* 1300, other slightly later), seventeenth-century communion rail.

ARKSEY ALL SAINTS   WR (SY) SE 5706
Norman cruciform church with crossing tower to which a spire was added in thirteenth century. Later modifications included north chapel (*c.* 1300) and south chapel, porch (with heraldic shields) and west front in Perp. period. There was a substantial restoration in 1870. Simple thirteenth-century sedilia, unusual font cover (1662), pulpit (1634), seventeenth-century pews. Fragments of medieval glass, mostly heraldic.

ARMTHORPE   WR (SY) SE 6105

ST MARY AND ST LEONARD
The restoration of 1885 produced the bell-turret, north aisle, east window and rendered exterior. In spite of this there is a Norman nave and chancel-arch and a thirteenth-century arch to support earlier bell-turret. Mass dial on south wall of chancel. Late nineteenth-century glass by Kempe. Unusual double title.

ARNCLIFFE ST OSWALD   WR (NY) SD 9371
Substantially remodelled in 1841 but tower (which retains fourteenth-century bell) and some windows are Perp. Church contains list of dalesmen who fought at Flodden Field (1513). Delightful setting.

ASKHAM BRYAN   ST NICHOLAS   WR (NY) SE 5548

Continuous nave and chancel with bell-cote. Late Norman, with good entrance and chancel. Reused Roman bricks in walls. Jacobean pulpit and communion rail. Fine situation.

ASKHAM RICHARD   ST MARY   WR (NY) SE 5347

So similar to Askham Bryan that one suspects same architect, but the original twelfth-century church was largely rebuilt in 1878. Porch contains slab which may be base of Norman churchyard cross. Pleasant late nineteenth-century panelled ceiling to chancel by Temple Moore. Kempe glass. Good eighteenth-century monument in churchyard.

ASKRIGG   ST OSWALD   NR (NY) SD 9490

Completely late Perp. and most impressive church in Wensleydale. No structural division between nave and chancel. Nave ceiling probably finest in NR. Interesting tower-vault. Eighteenth-century glass in north aisle. Unfortunate east window and perhaps not everyone will be happy about re-arranged chancel.

ASTON   ALL SAINTS   WR (SY) SK 4685

Late twelfth-century arcades, Dec. chancel and windows in south aisle. Attractive Perp. tower and south porch with statue niche. Font is Perp. but seated man at its foot is unique, and of mysterious import. Restructured Darcy monument of earlier seventeenth century.

AUGHTON   ALL SAINTS   ER (H) SK 4585

In close proximity to earthworks of Norman castle and later site of Aske moated manor. Norman chancel-arch much distorted, Norman font, restored Norman doorway. Nave widened in thirteenth century; tower (of unusual rectangular plan) added or modified in 1536 (date inscribed on south side with row of shields). Good large brass (1466+) of Richard Aske and his wife.

AUSTERFIELD   ST HELEN   WR (SY) SK 6594

Evidence of early Norman origins in south doorway (with rare tympanum), chancel-arch and font. North aisle is a later Norman addition (with equally rare fertility figure at corner of one capital). Thirteenth-century west front. Rustic Jacobean communion rail.

Kempe glass. Village and church have associations with 'Pilgrim Fathers'.

AYSGARTH   ST ANDREW   NR (NY) SE 0088
Distant from modern village and near river. Apart from lower part of tower, entirely rebuilt in 1866, yet it contains the best screen in NR, which has been repainted to something like its medieval splendour. Other fine woodwork includes a reading-desk made from two magnificent recycled bench ends. Together they bear the date 1536 and the initials A.S. which are taken to refer to Adam of Sedbergh, Abbot of Jervaulx, to which the church was appropriated. Interesting vestry cupboards. 'Good Samaritan' window commemorates donor's escape from burglars.

AYTON   ST JOHN BAPTIST   NR (NY) SE 9984
There might be A/S work in tower arch, there is Norman work in south doorway, chancel-arch and font. Chancel modified in thirteenth century and, together with nave, heavily buttressed in the fifteenth. East window inserted in eighteenth century (modern glass by Harry Stammers).

BADSWORTH   ST MARY   WR (WY) SE 4614
Largely Perp. but earlier work in reused Norman capital (south aisle wall), thirteenth-century north doorway, Dec. chancel with good windows. Perp. font (from Barnsley parish church). Good wall tablet (1688). Kempe glass (c. 1893, 1900 – with wheat-sheaf trademark).

BAINTON   ST ANDREW   ER (H) SE 9652
Rebuilt by rector in early fourteenth century, producing a rare uniform Dec. church (tower had spire until 1715). Font survives from Norman period. Remarkable Mauley monument resembling Percy tomb at Beverley. Goodeale brass (†1429). Two eighteenth-century pews.

BARDSEY   ALL HALLOWS   WR (WY) SE 3643
A/S tower, heightened and corbelled out in local fashion during Perp. period. Norman work in north arcade and reset south doorway. Dec. chancel (much renewed), aisles widened in Perp. period, north 'chapel' added in seventeenth century and south extension built as family pew in 1724.

BARMSTON ALL SAINTS   ER (H) TA 1569
Basically Norman structure of rubble and cobble with Perp.
modifications (windows and chancel arch). Fragments of a hog-back
tomb and medieval glass. Mid-fifteenth-century alabaster effigy on
tomb-chest. Imposing seventeenth-century Boynton monument.

BARNBURGH ST PETER   WR (SY) SE 4845
Norman tower with Perp. top and spirelet. Norman arcade (and
interesting cross-shaft fragments), Dec. chancel; rest largely Perp.
including battlements, south porch and screens. Curious aumbry at
west end but treasure is oaken effigy of cross-legged knight holding
his heart (dating from early fourteenth century) under canopy of
1477+. He is said to have fought a wild cat in church porch and both
were killed.

BARNBY DUN SS PETER AND PAUL   WR (SY) SE 6109
Apart from Perp. tower, almost completely Dec. (including
clerestory). Interesting rood stair. Though chancel was rebuilt (1860),
it retains internal and external niches, much of sedilia and piscina
(latter of a striking design). Perp. font and characteristic eighteenth-
century monuments.

BARNOLDSWICK ST MARY-LE-GILL   WR (L) SD 8746
Remote situation away from present town (now provided with a
nineteenth-century church). Perp. work of various times (date on
tower reads 1524), chancel earlier, nave and north aisle earlier still.
Font and holy-water stoup in porch possibly Norman. Three-decker
pulpit, Jacobean box pews.

BARTON-LE-STREET ST MICHAEL   NR (NY) SE 7274
Sumptuously rebuilt in Norman style in 1871 but may reflect
original. Some work is original Norman (buttresses and doorway)
though often reset. Details worth close examination both in porch
and inside church (pillar-piscina for example). Pevsner describes
doorways as 'amongst most exuberantly decorated in Yorkshire'.
Organ case designed by Temple Moore.

BARWICK-IN-ELMET ALL SAINTS   WR (WR) SE 3937
Apart from one Norman window (only visible from within chancel),

The spectacular late Perpendicular font cover at Bradford Cathedral (formerly the parish church of St Peter)

The monument to Sir William, died 1634, at St John's Knaresborough. The monument is attributed to Epiphanius Evesham

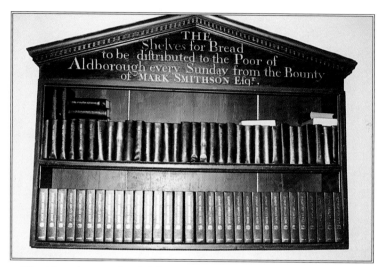

The eighteenth-century bread shelves at St Andrew, Aldborough, North Yorkshire

Hogback tombs at St Thomas, Brompton-in-Allertonshire, North Yorkshire

The south portal at St John Baptist Church, Adel, West Yorkshire

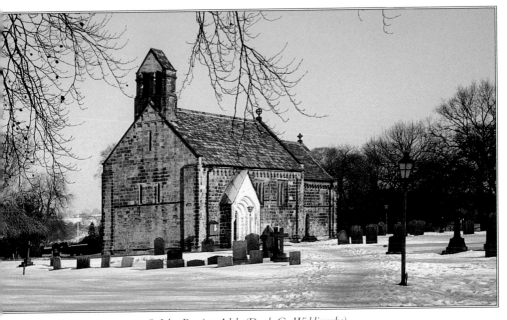

St John Baptist, Adel. (Derek G. Widdicombe)

St Michael, Haworth, West Yorkshire. (Derek G. Widdicombe (photo: Jacqui Rick))

All Saints, Mappleton, Humberside. (Derek G. Widdicombe (photo: Brian Jackson))

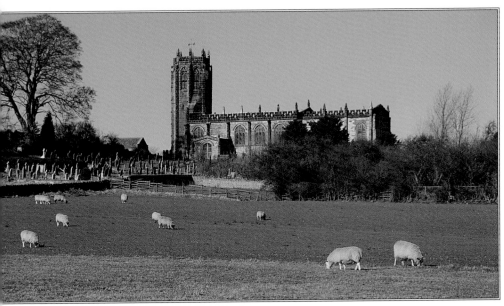

St Michael, Coxwold, North Yorkshire. (Derek G. Widdicombe (photo: Brian Jackson))

St Mary and St Germain, Selby, North Yorkshire. (Derek G. Widdicombe (photo: Dorothy Burrows))

St Oswald, Arncliffe, North Yorkshire. (Derek G. Widdicombe)

St Mary, Lastingham, North Yorkshire. (Derek G. Widdicombe (photo: Brian Jackson))

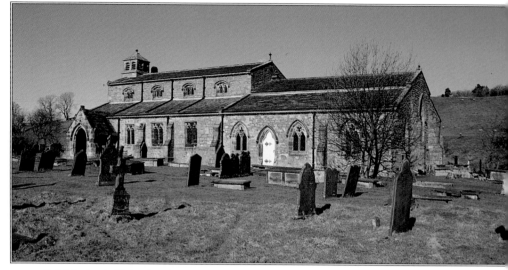

St Michael and All Angels, Linton, North Yorkshire. (Derek G. Widdicombe (photo: Dorothy Burrows))

Holy Trinity, Skipton, North Yorkshire. (Derek G. Widdicombe)

church dates from fourteenth century or later. Dec. style vestry doorway. Perp. aisles, arcades, clerestory and tower (with inscription and date 1455). Two late A/S cross fragments, good late Georgian pulpit. Motte of Norman castle in village.

BATLEY ALL SAINTS   WR (WY) SE 2424
Long, low 'typically WR', mainly Perp. but with Dec. south arcade and doorway. Rood stairs. Late fifteenth-century screen to North chapel. Mirfield monument (†1496): alabaster effigies on stone chest. Medieval glass fragments (south aisle). Standard 1662 font.

BAWTRY ST NICHOLAS   WR (SY) SK 6592
Originated as chapel-of-ease to Blyth when Bawtry was established as a 'new town' late in the twelfth century. Some work of c. 1300, more of Perp. period and later (repairs of seventeenth century, tower built in eighteenth century reusing some fourteenth-century material). Good eighteenth-century ironwork in south chapel (recycled garden gate).

BEDALE ST GREGORY   NR (NY) SE 2688
Apart from Perp. bell-stage of fine tower, a Dec. church of unusual design (the south porch, for example, is attached to tower) with unfortunate Victorian fenestration (the east window is said to be from Jervaulx). Perp. modifications included clerestory and south chapel. Crypt with interesting stone fragments. Good sedilia; recycled panelling round altar (from the sixteenth and seventeenth centuries); wall-painting on chancel arch and north wall of aisle. Several effigies including very early alabaster. Internal tower stair once protected by portcullis. Poor-box.

BEEFORD ST LEONARD   ER (H) TA 1254
Almost entirely Perp., including fine tower which retains statue of patron. EE windows in chancel. Fourteenth-century effigy of priest and brass of former rector (†1472).

BEIGHTON ST MARY   (SY) SK 4183
Originally Norman, and largely rebuilt in Perp. period and restored 1868. Fine Perp. tower, fragments of medieval glass. Nineteenth-century Italian reredos in alabaster, later rood by Comper.

BEMPTON ST MICHAEL   ER (H) TA 1972
Much EE work including font. Interesting upper stage of tower. Brick chancel (1829) and unusual screen incorporating Royal Arms (possibly dating from the late eighteenth century). Clerestory constructed in 1906.

BEVERLEY ST MARY   ER (H) TA 0339
Considered one of most beautiful parish churches in England. Some fragments of Norman, a little more of EE (late thirteenth-century north transept chapel with crypt), but essentially Perp. work of fourteenth to early sixteenth centuries. Magnificent west front, outstanding porch and splendid tower (1520–30). Nave piers record benefactors (including famous minstrels). Superb woodwork includes early fifteenth-century stalls (with misericords). Roughly contemporary painted ceiling is unique (though twice repainted). Fine early sixteenth-century ceiling in north chancel chapel. Richly carved font of Derbyshire marble was given in 1530. Rare 'Priests Room' above sacristy, approached by ingeniously designed spiral stairs, has heterogeneous collection of fragments and ecclesiastical bygones.

BILTON AINSTEY ST HELEN   WR (NY) SE 4749
Late Norman with impressive west front. EE arcades and Perp. chancel chapels. Restoration in 1869. Interesting fragments of A/S crosses. Much restored eagle lectern in wood (c. 1500). Early fourteenth-century monument (defaced) possibly to abbess of Sinningthwaite.

BINGLEY ALL SAINTS   WR (WY) SE 1039
Generally Perp. impression with nineteenth-century restoration (including tower top). A/S fragment, impressive Norman (or possibly earlier) font with runic inscription, late nineteenth-century chancel screen. Twentieth-century organ case and other furnishing by G.G. Pace.

Holy Trinity, at other end of town, is a notable church by Norman Shaw (1868) with excellent chancel and good Morris stained glass.

BIRDFORTH ST MARY (R)   NR (NY) SE 4875
A puzzling church, now in care of Redundant Churches Fund.

Possibly Norman originally, remodelled in late sixteenth century (panel in chancel with 1585 date). Jacobean font cover, seventeenth-century pulpit. Victorian brick turret.

BIRDSALL   ST MARY   ER (NY) SE 8165
Built in 1823 with chancel of 1881. Preserves monuments from old church including fourteenth-century effigy of lady and good tablets dating from the seventeenth, eighteenth and early nineteenth centuries. Some glass of 1903.

Ruined old church, close to Big House, retains Norman chancel-arch, thirteenth-century arcades and later tower (possibly dated 1601).

BIRKIN   ST MARY   WR (NY) SE 5226
One of most impressive Norman churches in Yorkshire. Its quality has been related to an association with the Templars. Dec. south aisle added c. 1330 and tower heightened in Perp. period. Excellent south doorway and fine apse. Font 1663. Eighteenth-century pulpit with tester. Some fourteenth-century glass in east window of south aisle. Good early fourteenth-century effigy of civilian. Monument to royalist vicar describing his misfortunes in Civil War.

BIRSTALL   ST PETER   WR (WY) SE 2226
Rebuilt 1870 but some earlier features remain: Norman tower with Perp. top, bench ends of early sixteenth and early seventeenth centuries, sculptural fragments (eleventh-century cross-base, twelfth-century coffin lid), shroud brass of Mrs Copeley (†1623). Nineteenth-century glass.

BISHOP BURTON   ALL SAINTS   ER (H) SE 9839
Unusual thirteenth-century tower with north and south doorways and access to nave. EE chancel is nineteenth-century reproduction (good vestry staircase). Nave has Dec. details but is also nineteenth-century rebuild. Fragment of Norman churchyard cross-head. Chalice brass (†1460), Ellerker brass (†1579). Alabaster effigy in shroud (†1684). Finely carved pew ends. Bust of John Wesley in elm wood.

BISHOP WILTON   ST EDITH   ER (H) SE 7955
Good nineteenth-century restoration preserving Norman (chancel-arch, south doorway), Dec. (windows), and Perp. (tower and spire)

work. Fine nineteenth-century hammer-beam roof, font and cover (1902) by Temple Moore who also designed unusual flooring. Remarkable brass and iron chancel-screen of late nineteenth century (Street). Title is rare commemoration of tenth-century nun of Wilton Abbey, Wilts., which once owned the medieval manor.

BOLTON ABBEY WR (NY) SE 0753

BLESSED VIRGIN AND ST CUTHBERT
Fragment of dissolved Austin priory (nave of church) retained in Anglican parochial use. Fine EE work with exceptional west façade obscured by later tower (begun 1520 but completion halted by Suppression in 1539). East end consists of wall built when monastic quire was ruined (nineteenth-century tracery and painted decoration). Interesting details include medieval mensa, bosses, old font, a few medieval tiles and other fragments. Title combines patron of original (Easby) and later Augustinian houses.

BOLTON-BY-BOWLAND WR (L) SD 7849

SS PETER AND PAUL
Some thirteenth-century work, but Perp. impression overall (mid-nineteenth-century restoration). Impressive Perp. font of early sixteenth century. Late seventeenth-century pews, early eighteenth-century communion rail and panel from former pulpit (later pulpit has Flemish reliefs). Remarkable Pudsey tomb of late fifteenth century: large incised marble slab depicting husband, three wives and twenty-five children. Small brass of 1509+.

BOLTON-ON-DEARNE   ST ANDREW   WR (SY) SE 4502
Traces of A/S masonry on nave exterior, EE north arcade, Dec. North chapel, east window, north doorway. Perp. south window. All much renewed. Eighteenth-century pulpit with marquetry. Rood of 1955.

BOLTON-ON-SWALE   ST MARY   NR (NY) SE 2599
Main feature is the big tower (possibly dated late sixteenth century). South arcade may be from the thirteenth century, and the rest from the later nineteenth. Tile-work and wall-painting of 1877. Curious

nineteenth-century Carpenter monument, interesting eighteenth-century tablets concerning Henry Jenkins (†1670, aged 169), and Grammar School headmaster.

BOLTON PERCY   ALL SAINTS   WR (NY) SE 5341
Fine large Perp. church built 1411–23 by its rector, Thomas Parker, and consecrated in 1424. Spacious interior with beautiful chancel retaining medieval return stalls and glass in east window. Jacobean box pews, eighteenth-century pulpit with tester (Jacobean predecessor cut down to make reader's desk). Monuments include Fairfax (†1648) and Miller (1807). Medieval (east window) and Kempe glass. Churchyard has Eliz. ornament (possibly a sundial).

BOSSALL   ST BOTOLPH   NR (NY) SE 7160
Cruciform church of Trans. period. Fine south doorway and simpler, matching one to north. EE chancel, tower heightened in Perp. period. Unusual font of, possibly, the twelfth century with seventeenth-century cover. Royal Arms (1710). Brass (1454+) and seventeenth-century Bolt monuments. Kempe glass. Title remembers seventh-century monastic founder who gave his name to this village and Boston, Lincolnshire.

BOWES   ST GILES   NR (D) NY 9913
Unsympathetic restoration of 1865 inserted windows and produced general nineteenth-century appearance to exterior. Norman north and south doorways, fourteenth-century transepts, Perp. east window and porch (crucifixion over entrance). Two fonts (Norman and EE). Roman inscription (c. AD 205). Curious stone at back of piscina and unusual coffin lid. Churchyard has 1822 monument to schoolboy who died at Bowes Academy (original of Dickens' *Dotheboys Hall*).

BOYNTON   ST ANDREW   ER (H) TA 1368
Perp. tower, brick nave and chancel of 1770 by John Carr with doubled chancel-arch and iron railing for screen. Family pew under tower, turkey lectern, seventeenth- to eighteenth-century monuments. Peckitt glass of the eighteenth century.

BRACEWELL   ST MICHAEL   WR (L) SD 8648
Norman doorway, chancel-arch, font and most of tower. Perp.

remodelling produced continuous roof over nave, aisle and chapels. Statue niches in nave arcades. Jacobean pulpit.

BRADFIELD ST NICHOLAS   WR (SY) SK 2692
One of largest churches in Hallamshire. Dec. tower and east window of North chapel. Rest Perp. (reused earlier material in arcades and chancel-arch) including fine nave roof. Former vestry (?), with fireplace, east of south chapel. Nineteenth-century reredos incorporates medieval panels from Caen. Early cross-head. Late medieval glass in north windows. Seventeenth-century brass. Rare eighteenth-century watch-house near churchyard gate.

BRADFORD ST PETER   WR (WY) SE 1633
Parish church until 1919. Fourteenth-century nave arcade but rest Perp. apart from twentieth-century extensions. Spectacular font cover (Perp.), fragments include A/S carving, coffin cover, etc. Fine Morris glass of 1862. Many large eighteenth-century monuments, those of nineteenth-century include Priestley and Sharp.

BRAFFERTON ST PETER   WR (NY) SE 4370
Unusual rebuilding of 1826–31 involved insertion of new nave between Perp. tower and Perp. chancel and chapels (Nevile foundations). Thirteenth-century coffin cover of prior of Newburgh (to which church was appropriated). Medieval inscriptions in chapels, fragmentary old glass, good eighteenth-century wall tablet (Turner). Kempe glass.

BRAITHWELL ST JAMES   WR (SY) SK 5394
Norman doorway with primitive tympanum, EE chancel-arch with associated work implying planned central tower. Early fourteenth-century (Dec.) chancel, several Perp. windows and west tower. Eliz. panels in pulpit (one dated 1574).

BRAMHAM ALL SAINTS   WR (WY) SE 4242
Much renewed Norman tower with Perp. top (including spire). Mostly EE apart from nineteenth-century chancel chapels. The interesting corbelled-out battlements on south wall of nave are Perp. Unusual twentieth-century screen-work and panelling in chancel.

BRANDESBURTON ST MARY   ER (H) TA 1147
Largely of the thirteenth century apart from reset Norman priest's doorway. Much early (fourteenth-century) brickwork. Nice Perp. niche in north-east corner of low (possibly thirteenth-century) tower. St Quintin brass (†1397), demi. to priest (†1364) (both damaged).

BRANDSBY ALL SAINTS   NR (NY) SK 8979
Very attractive small church of 1770, crowned with open cupola. West porch added in 1913 and later twentieth-century nave panelling by Thompson of Kiburn. Elegant eighteenth-century font. Small crude crucifixion, probably Norman.

BRAYTON ST WILFRID   WR (NY) SE 6030
Fine tall Norman tower with added Perp. octagon and slender spire. Rich Norman south doorway but details badly weathered. Dec. chancel (with handsome sedilia and piscina) and aisle arcades. Perp. windows including clerestory. Darcy monument (†1558), now headless.

BRIDLINGTON ST MARY   ER (H) TA 1766
Fragment of great Austin priory retained in parochial use. Impressive thirteenth- to fourteenth-century work in interior, Western towers restored with additions in 1870s. Fourteenth-century font of Frosterley marble, unusual pillar piscina possibly of Perp. period. Monuments include impressive twelfth-century Tournai marble slab with animals etc. (possibly to founder), splendid ledger stone of +1671 and Hebblethwaite sarcophagus (†1773).

BRODSWORTH ST MICHAEL   WR (SY) SE 5007
Norman nave and one window. Trans. north aisle, thirteenth-century tower, south doorway, chancel. Nineteenth-century south aisle and family chapel. Good carved pulpit of 1696.

BROMPTON ALL SAINTS   NR (NY) SE 9482
Large church with tower and broach spire (Dec.). Thirteenth-century north doorway, rest mainly Perp. South door has traceried work of Perp. period. Interesting sculptures of thirteenth and fourteenth centuries outside chapel. Chancel south window of c. 1885 is a version of a Raphael painting in Sistine Chapel. Many eighteenth-

and nineteenth-century monuments (porch is memorial to Sir George Cayley (†1853), the 'father of aeronautics').

BROMPTON-IN-ALLERTONSHIRE   NR (NY) SE 3796

ST THOMAS
Much restored in 1868 but retains combined porch and tower of Perp. period. Late twelfth-century arcade and fine collection of A/D sculpture, including three excellent hog-backs.

BROUGHTON   ALL SAINTS   WR (NY) SE 7673
Largely rebuilt in Perp. period with squat west tower and nave, chancel and north aisle under single low roof. Norman south doorway and font survives from earlier church (and evidence of window and former priest's doorway). Perp. parclose screen to North chapel and remains of alabaster statues of Blessed Virgin Mary (of the fifteenth and early sixteenth centuries).

BUBWITH   ALL SAINTS   ER (H) SE 7136
Largish church, originally Norman, aisles added and chancel enlarged in the thirteenth century. Handsome tower, extension of nave, clerestory, external pinnacles and battlements were contributed in Perp. period (as was inscribed font). Fragments of medieval glass. Jacobean work in pews. Funeral helm and sword in north-east corner.

BUGTHORPE   ST ANDREW   ER (H) SE 7757
Originally Norman, extended c. 1300 and tower added in fourteenth century. North chapel rebuilt 1905. Incomplete reconstruction has left church with two chancel arches and earlier one has very interesting Norman carving. Good modern furnishing including rare canopy over altar. Monuments include coffin lid with foliated crosses and more ostentatious examples from the seventeenth and eighteenth centuries. Unusual feature is stair turret with spire to north of chancel.

BULMER   ST MARTIN   NR (NY) SE 6967
Nave may be late A/S. Late twelfth-century doorway and font. Perp. tower and North chapel (now ruined), chancel arch. Chancel rebuilt 1898. Head of A/S cross, late thirteenth-century effigy (legs missing).

Porch has eighteenth-century memorial to master-smith of Castle Howard.

BURGHWALLIS   ST HELEN   WR (SY) SE 5312
Early Norman nave and tower. Much herring-bone work. Chancel-arch and chancel possibly of thirteenth century. South porch may be from same period. Medieval hinges on door. First-class Perp. rood-screen (well restored 1881, rood added later). Gascoigne brass (†1554). Victorian reredos in alabaster (lately recoloured).

BURNBY   ST GILES   ER (H) SE 8346
Norman and EE (lost north aisle and north chapel). Chancel rebuilt in 1583 but has EE sedilia and piscina (reputedly from Warter priory) and remarkable low side window of *c.* 1300. More rebuilding in 1840s (west end) and 1908 (roof). Thirteenth-century ironwork on priest's door.

BURNESTON   ST LAMBERT   NR (NY) SE 3084
Entirely in Perp. style, battlements, pinnacles, clerestory, large windows, sedilia, etc. Chancel-arch badly damaged (possibly when screen was removed), font dated 1662. Complete set of pews, culminating in three-tiered family pew, made in 1627 for £50. Title commemorates seventh-century missionary bishop of Maastricht martyred in 700.

BURNSALL   ST WILFRID   WR (NY) SE 0361
Perp. apart from two windows in south chapel. Later modifications in 1612. Crude Norman font, fifteenth-century alabaster panel, Jacobean pulpit, many A/S fragments, two hog-backs, stocks in churchyard entered by delightful lych-gate (possibly of the late seventeenth century).

BURSTWICK   ALL SAINTS   ER (H) TA 2228
Work from late twelfth to fourteenth centuries and after. Sedile of fourteenth century, tower and north arcade later (Perp. features). Rare Royal Arms with painting on reverse of execution of Charles I, presented to church in 1676.

BURTON AGNES   ST MARTIN   ER (H) TA 1063
Appears Perp. at first glance (tower, clerestory, battlements) but

actually basically Norman, with EE south arcade, and Dec. window in north aisle. Brick repairs to chancel in the eighteenth century and rebuilding in 1840. Retooled Norman font, pulpit *c.* 1700, monumental Boynton family pew, early Georgian box pews. Rare eighteenth-century glass. Numerous monuments from the fifteenth to eighteenth centuries.

BURTON FLEMING   ST CUTHBERT   ER (H) TA 0872
Much altered Norman church of which doorway, font (with carved heads), part of chancel-arch, tower, remain. External evidence of lost Norman aisle. Plain interior.

BURTON PIDSEA   ST PETER   ER (H) TA 2431
Cobble and rubble with brick east end of 1838. Mainly Perp. (good south doorway, windows, arcade) but one EE and one Dec. window. Later fifteenth-century tower built into aisles.

CALVERLEY   ST WILFRID   WR (WY) SE 2036
Large church, mainly Dec. in style but evidence of Norman origins in nave and Perp. period added tower top and clerestory. Very good Jacobean font cover, meagre fragments of medieval glass (east window).

CAMPSALL   ST MARY MAGDALENE   WR (SY) SE 5313
Large cruciform church, mainly Norman of two builds, with EE, Dec., and Perp. additions and modifications. Fine west end with most ambitious Norman tower in WR. West bay of south aisle (*c.* 1300) is vaulted with a chamber above. EE sedilia and more primitive predecessor. Fine Dec. south doorway. Perp. windows and clerestory, porch, pinnacles and battlements. Substantial remains of fifteenth-century rood-screen (compare Hatfield) with rhymed inscription. Flaxman monument to Yarborough family (1803). Altar (from nearby hall) by Pugin. Old vicarage is a fifteenth-century manor-house.

CANTLEY   ST WILFRID   WR (SY) SE 6202
Norman priest's door, some EE windows and doorway. Dec. contribution included north chapel (lost) and south arcade. Perp. tower. North arcade and aisle (1894) by Ninian Comper who also provided rood-screen, parclose screen, altar furnishings, etc., all coloured in medieval manner.

CARLTON HUSTHWAITE ST MARY   NR (NY) SE 4976
Very small and simple country church of seventeenth century.
Perfectly preserved interior of period includes two-decker pulpit
(1678) with tester, complete set of stalls and benches, and communion
rail.

CARNABY ST JOHN BAPTIST   ER (H) TA 1465
Stone and much brick. Norman font, EE windows (paired lancets
illustrating development of plate tracery), south arcade, tower
(heightened in Perp. period). Latin inscription on a south pier records
the nearby burial of Walter Uppiby.

CASTLE BOLTON ST OSWALD   NR (NY) SE 0391
Modest church in shadow of immodest castle (which possessed private
collegiate chapel). Late fourteenth-century work with no division
between nave and chancel (unusual for period). Low side window,
unusual sedilia, high corbels which may have carried rood-beam (part
survives in tower), nave piscina. Mass dial east of porch.

CATTERICK ST ANNE   NR (NY) SE 2397
Contract survives for this church built in 1412. North chapel (1491)
and south chapel (1505), clerestory (1872). Workmanship (including
sedilia) somewhat rustic but fine black marble font. Contemporary
parclose screen to south chapel. Later fourteenth-century effigy of
swordless knight, three Burgh brasses (of the fifteenth century). Rare
dedication commemorates mother of Blessed Virgin Mary.

CAWOOD ALL SAINTS   WR (NY) SE 5737
Fine battlemented and pinnacled Perp. tower (with image niche),
unusually placed at west end of south aisle. Late Norman doorways
(south and west), EE chancel (destroyed south chapel), many Perp.
windows (one with fragments of contemporary glass). Monument to
Archbishop Mountain (†1623). (Church and manor belonged to
archbishops of York.)

CAWTHORNE ALL SAINTS   WR (SY) SE 2807
Almost entirely rebuilt in 1880, reusing some EE work. Other
survivals include north chapel (of the thirteenth century), windows of
north aisle (Perp., as is tower). Two fonts: one Norman, other Perp.

Perp. tomb-chest, some good tablets, pre-Raphaelite stained glass (and pulpit panels).

CAYTON   ST JOHN BAPTIST   NR (NY) TA 0583
Norman church (south doorway and north arcade) with heavily buttressed, unusually squat Perp. tower. All windows were replaced in the nineteenth century. Reredos contains a relief said to be sixteenth-century Flemish work.

CHAPEL-LE-DALE   ST LEONARD   WR (NY) SD 7377
Former chapel-of-ease to Ingleton, wholly rebuilt in the seventeenth century and partly renewed in 1869. Wall tablet commemorates those killed in constructing Settle–Carlisle railway (completed 1876). (St Leonard was a Frankish hermit of the sixth century whose cult became very popular in the twelfth century. He was the patron saint of prisoners, especially those taken in war.)

CHURCH FENTON   ALL SAINTS   WR (NY) SE 5136
Essentially EE cruciform church (tower rebuilt in the fifteenth century). Many Dec. windows and some fragments of fourteenth-century glass. Perp. screen. Early fourteenth-century effigy of lady: hands in prayer, lion and demon at her feet fight over cat.

COLLINGHAM   ST OSWALD   WR (WY) SE 3845
Apart from Perp. tower, exterior reflects heavy restoration of 1841 but some of fabric may be A/S. North arcade c. 1200 and aisle Perp. Important remains of A/S crosses: one c. 800 (with figures of apostles), other of late ninth century (with dragons and runes). Rare cresset stone.

CONISBROUGH   ST PETER   WR (SY) SK 5098
Evidence of A/S work but present form largely of the late twelfth century (capitals of north arcade worth close inspection). Some Dec. work (east window of north aisle), Perp. tower top and clerestory. Twentieth-century north chapel. A/S cross fragment, remarkable richly-carved twelfth-century tomb-chest, thirteenth-century pillar piscina, good Perp. font, fragments of fifteenth-century glass (interesting eighteenth-century work in small windows, as well as nineteenth- to twentieth-century glass).

CONISTONE ST MARY   WR (NY) SD 9867
Though largely rebuilt in 1846, St Mary's is reputedly the oldest
church in Craven, possibly with A/S origins and certainly with
original Norman work in nave arcade as well as Perp. Wall tablets.

COPGROVE ST MICHAEL   WR (NY) SE 3463
Maintains simple Norman two-cell plan with bell-cote. Retains some
original features (Norman window, chancel-arch and figure on north-
east corner of vestry wall). Much restored.

COTTINGHAM ST MARY   ER (H) TA 0532
Fine cruciform church with dominant Perp. crossing-tower (nave
largely Dec., chancel and transepts Perp.). Large brass to Nicholas de
Luda (†1384), Franciscan friar who had chancel built while he was
rector. Two small brasses of early sixteenth century, grandiose
eighteenth-century monuments, others of earlier nineteenth-century.
Much nineteenth-century French stained glass (Capronnier).

COVERHAM HOLY TRINITY   NR (NY) SE 0886
Fine, remote position in Coverdale. Probably A/S site but present
church, over-restored in 1855, preserves nothing earlier than EE
(chancel). South aisle of early fourteenth century. Later alterations in
sixteenth and seventeenth centuries. A/S stone over south door.
Victorian tiling and armorial glass.

COWLAM ST MARY   ER (H) SE 9665
Unpretentious building of 1852 but retains remarkable Norman font
with copious figure-carving whose total significance is somewhat
mysterious. Tablets include one ascribed to Chantrey (Foord-Bowes
†1839).

COWTHORPE ST MICHAEL (R)   WR (NY) SE 4252
Built in 1450s with west tower of unique form. Remains (?) of
Rowcliffe brass, commemorating builder of church. Remarkable
survival of oak Easter Sepulchre. Fragments of contemporary glass in
tracery heads. Jacobean communion rail.

COXWOLD ST MICHAEL   NR (NY) SE 5377
Essentially a fifteenth-century church with distinctive octagonal

tower. Chancel rebuilt 1774 and serves chiefly as receptacle for Bellasis monuments (south window of 1912). Nave ceiling has (reset) bosses. Communion rail of early eighteenth century takes unique form. Pulpit, box pews, west gallery probably all of eighteenth century. Some fifteenth-century glass in tracery heads. Hanoverian Royal Arms. Monument to Laurence Sterne (incumbent 1760–8) in churchyard.

CRAMBE   ST MICHAEL   NR (NY) SE 7364
Early Norman, nave lengthened in thirteenth century, Perp. tower in different stone. (Tower-arch worth inspection.) Late Norman font, Jacobean pulpit, some good wall tablets.

CRATHORNE   ALL SAINTS   NR (NY) NZ 4407
Nineteenth-century tower and chancel, Norman work in nave and A/D (possibly ninth-century) work in porch lintel and fragments. Effigies include rare (but unrecognizable) deacon and fourteenth-century cross-legged knight.

CRAYKE   ST CUTHBERT   NR (NY) SE 5670
Characteristically Perp. (with battlements and pinnacles), apart from nineteenth-century north aisle. Perp. screen, Jacobean pews and pulpit with tester (1637), A/S cross fragments (*c.* 800), sixteenth-century recumbent effigies. Two ancient chests. St Cuthbert's body rested here for a time before it came to rest in Durham.

CROFT   ST PETER   NR (NY) NZ 2909
Norman origins (lower tower), much EE work (chancel) with substantial modifications in fourteenth and fifteenth centuries (including upper tower). Highly ornate, but somewhat crude, sedilia, etc., fifteenth-century parclose screen, late seventeenth-century communion rail and presumptuous Milbanke family pew, eighteenth-century font. Clervaux tomb-chests and seventeenth-century Milbanke. Eighteenth-century Milbanke tablet. Fine A/S fragment. Curious figure by door (possibly Romano-British).

CROFTON   ALL SAINTS   WR (WY) SE 3717
Cruciform with crossing-tower, rebuilt for his birthplace by Bishop Fleming of Lincoln (†1431). Interesting A/S cross fragments.

DALBY   ST PETER   NR (NY) SE 6371
Two-cell plan with bell-cote, retaining Norman doorway and
chancel-arch. Remodelled in fifteenth century which produced
remarkable chancel with tunnel-vault and external appearance of
fortification.

DANBY   ST HILDA   NR (NY) NZ 7008
Nave rebuilt 1789, chancel in 1848 (restored 1903), sparse Norman
remains but south porch tower is an unusual and modest Perp. piece.

DANBY WISKE   TITLE UNKNOWN   NR (NY) SE 3398
Norman south doorway with tympanum *in situ*. EE work in north
arcade, Dec. chancel, fine Perp. tower and clerestory. Early
fourteenth-century effigy (entirely retooled). Stalls with recycled
Jacobean panels. Title presumably lost in Reformation turmoil.

DARFIELD   ALL SAINTS   WR (SY) SE 4104
Norman tower with Perp. top. Perp. north chapel; rest mainly Dec.
South aisle has attractive painted ceiling (eighteenth century). Perp.
font with Jacobean cover. Jacobean communion rails in chancel and
south chapel, with contemporary benches rising in tiers under tower.
Family pew in chancel reuses medieval bench ends. Alabaster effigies
(*c*. 1400). Churchyard has monument to colliery disaster of 1857.

DARRINGTON   ST LUKE AND ALL SAINTS WR (WY) SE 4919
Sturdy Norman tower with Perp. top, embraced by thirteenth-
century aisles. Chancel also EE. Dec. windows, south doorways and
perhaps porch, chancel-arch and north chapel. Perp. east window.
Unique rood stair-turret and access gallery. Some Perp. stalls (with
misericords) and bench ends. Defaced sculpture of horseman and St
Andrew (both 'brought in' ?). Fifteenth-century glass fragments. Two
good fourteenth-century effigies. Farrer (†1684) monument of
mounted ledger stone. Remains of eighteenth-century dove-cote in
churchyard. Unusual (altered?) title.

DARTON   ALL SAINTS   WR (SY) SE 3110
Entirely Perp. (chancel provided by Monk Bretton priory in 1517).
Contemporary roofs in nave and chancel, Perp. parclose screens and
rare early sixteenth-century stained glass of St Mary Magdalene

(patron of priory). Communion rail *c.* 1700 with fashionable central projection. Italian Baroque painting. Silvester tomb (†1722).

DENT   ST ANDREW   WR (C) SD 7087
Essentially late Perp. but blocked Norman doorway and EE survivals in nave arcades. Seventeenth-century pews, font-cover and parts of pulpit, eighteenth-century tower and a good deal of restoration in 1889. Chancel floored in various local marbles.

DENTON   ST HELEN   WR (WY) SE 1448
Medieval church replaced in 1776 to match new hall (both built by John Carr). Rare example of eighteenth-century 'Gothick'. The east window (Gyles, 1700) is characteristic work of period (translated from replaced hall). Pleasant interior with nice furnishings.

DEWSBURY   ALL SAINTS   WR (WY) SE 2422
EE work survives eighteenth-century and 1895 rebuilding. Many A/S sculptural pieces of ninth century, some important. Other remains include unusual hog-back and fine thirteenth-century coffin lid. North transept window has worthwhile fragments of thirteenth- and fourteenth-century glass.

DOWNHOLME   ST MICHAEL   NE (NY) SE 1197
Norman south doorway and arcade; EE north aisle, chancel-arch; Dec. east window and porch. Eighteenth-century window. Norman font converted to 'Perp.' in nineteenth-century. Grave slabs in porch.

DRAX   SS PETER AND PAUL   WR (NY) SE 6726
Norman work of three builds, EE chancel, Dec. south doorway and north chapel. Perp. top to tower (including bell-openings and spire) and fine battlements. Remarkable Perp. clerestory with shafts supported on well-carved figures. Good set of bench ends (early sixteenth century) with mixed medieval and Renaissance designs.

DUNNINGTON   ST NICHOLAS   ER (NY) SE 6652
Early Norman tower, later Norman nave arcades; good EE work in chancel including sedilia, piscina and arcade to north chapel. Much Victorian restoration including nave windows.

EASBY   ST AGATHA   NR (NY) NZ 1800
Uniquely situated within precinct of Premonstratensian abbey which
it antedates (some Norman work). Only simple bell-cote breaks line
of long, low slated roof. Mainly EE but south aisle and remarkable
porch date from fifteenth century. Chancel-arch is Victorian. Fine
wall-painting and other decoration survives from thirteenth century.
Cast of excellent A/S cross. Norman font. Some fourteenth-century
glass in east window.

EASINGTON   ALL SAINTS   ER (H) TA 3919
North doorway and pillar piscina are Norman, nave is EE, tower and
chancel Perp. Tower has grotesque called 'Easington imp'. Good wall
tablet of 1651.

EASINGWOLD   ALL SAINTS AND ST JOHN   NR (NY) SE 5269
Away from old town centre, 'typical North Country'. General Perp.
impression but north doorway is c. 1200, some windows and old west
doorway are Dec. Good tablet of 1713. Church still possesses a parish
coffin. Unusual 'double' title (probably altered).

EAST HARLSEY   ST OSWALD   NR (NY) SE 4299
Largely restoration of 1885 but bell-cote and south porch seem to
date from seventeenth century, as does communion rail. Fine effigy of
early fourteenth-century knight (face recut). Two interesting coffin
lids. Twentieth-century font (stone beaker shape with inset copper
bowl). Fine later seventeenth-century dove-cote in churchyard (north
of church).

EAST MARTON   ST PETER   WR (NY) SD 9050
Short, broad tower and some fragments are Norman, rest largely of
the nineteenth century. Brilliant A/D sculpture in tenth-century(?)
cross fragment.

EASTRINGTON   ST MICHAEL   ER (H) SE 7930
A good deal of Norman work (for example, frieze in north porch),
not always in situ, with an EE chancel aisle. Much seventeenth-
century rebuilding due to collapse of chancel in 1632. Some Dec.
windows. Perp. work includes clerestory and tower. Fourteenth-
century glass fragments. Fifteenth-century aisle roof, incised slab,

alabaster effigies: one combining armour with judicial robes. Seventeenth-century font cover.

EBBERSTON   ST MARY   NR (NY) SE 8983

Norman church, chancel modified in thirteenth century. South chapel added later (demolished after Reformation), tower from fourteenth or fifteenth century. Much rebuilding in late nineteenth century. Twelfth-century ironwork on (modern) door.

ECCLESFIELD   ST MARY   WR (SY) SK 3393

Large cruciform church whose size reflects extent of medieval parish. Ambitious Perp. structure using some older material. Fine original timber roofs in chancel chapels. Font dated 1662, less utilitarian than usual. Parclose and chancel-screens, return stalls with two misericords. Early sixteenth-century benches in south chapel with 'orate' (request for prayers). Some medieval glass, extensive Victorian sample from *c.* 1885 to 1895. A/S cross-shaft. Scott memorial of 1640. Militaria of early nineteenth century. Churchyard has grave of Nelson's naval chaplain (A.J. Scott).

EDLINGTON   WR (SY) SK 5397

ST PETER (OLD CHURCH) (R)

Trans. with much late Norman carving. EE chancel. North chapel, many windows and tower are Perp. Rare Eliz. (1590) font (and cover). Medieval bench ends (and pulpit?). Restored by Redundant Churches Fund in 1970s.

ELLAND   ST MARY   WR (WY) SE 1020

Perp. but some material reused from late twelfth century. Tower embraced by aisles; chancel chapels. East window contains much original glass of *c.* 1480 depicting life of Blessed Virgin Mary. Medieval fragments in west window of north aisle. Also Kempe glass. Horton wall monument of earlier eighteenth century, nineteenth-century Nichols monument.

ELLERBURN   ST HILDA   NR (NY) SE 8484

Beautifully sited little church of *c.* 1150 with EE window and (lost) south chapel of fifteenth century. Remains of A/S crosses. Norman font. Eighteenth-century pulpit and pews. Obtrusive Dobson monument (1879) in churchyard.

ELLOUGHTON   ST MARY   ER (H) SE 9428
EE doorway, Perp. tower. Rest 1846 (by Pearson) and restoration after 1964 fire. Saxon fragment in north wall of chancel. (Pulpit approach is Pearson mannerism.)

EMLEY   ST MICHAEL   WR (WY) SE 2413
Norman nave (door tympanum reset in south wall inside). Much extended in Perp. period (including fine tower and nave roof). Restoration font, eighteenth-century pulpit with tester, some box pews. Substantial fragments of fifteenth-century glass. Chandelier. Miner's lamp. Churchyard wall has stone with Maltese Cross, said to be from local Hospitaller dependency.

ERYHOLME   ST MARY   NR (NY) NZ 3208
North arcade *c.* 1200, nave EE, chancel of thirteenth century and tower of thirteenth or fourteenth century. A/D sculpture (?), coffin lid, 1930s glass.

ETTON   ST MARY   ER (H) SE 9743
Largely 1846 'Norman' rebuild but much original late twelfth-century work may be discovered: lower tower, south doorway, detached panels (from Holme-on-Wolds). South aisle and effigy of *c.* 1300. Royal Arms (unusual example carved in stone) above tower arch.

EVERINGHAM   ST EVERILDA   ER (H) SE 8042
EE tower, heightened in Perp. period. Rest rebuilt in brick *c.* 1763 probably by John Carr. Nearby hall has proud Catholic chapel (1836–9) with spectacular interior in which is preserved an early Norman font with much carving (from medieval parish church). Rare dedication commemorates seventh-century Wessex lady who is supposed to have established a nunnery in this area.

FANGFOSS   ST MARTIN   ER (H) SE 7653
Rebuilt 1850 but using much original Norman masonry, for example, buttresses, south doorway, frieze in chancel, corbel-table.

FARLINGTON ST LEONARD   NR (NY) SE 6167
Small Norman church of *c.* 1200 with Victorian bell-cote. Windows of various dates (including Victorian lancets).

FARNHAM ST OSWAL   WR (NY) SE 3640
Norman church of which beautiful chancel remains. Nave lost through added aisles (north, *c.* 1200; south, *c.* 1300) with extensions in fourteenth and fifteenth centuries and later addition of tower. Chancel-arch is 1854.

FEATHERSTONE ALL SAINTS   WR (WY) SE 4222
Heavily restored in Victorian period but older work survives, notably Perp. south porch, aisle and south chapel. Also font of same period with inscription.

FELIXKIRK ST FELIX   NR (NY) SE 4684
Norman church of *c.* 1125 (with possible Hospitaller associations), fairly accurately restored in 1860. Perp. tower. Fragments of medieval glass (*c.* 1300), effigies (retooled?) of same period. Felix was a Burgundian who became the apostle of East Anglia and gave his name to Felixstowe.

FELKIRK ST PETER   WR (WY) SE 4785
Originally Norman but much altered in EE and Perp. periods (latter work includes chancel chapels, south porch and tower). One bench has late sixteenth-century inlay.

FERRYBRIDGE ST ANDREW   WR (WY) SE 4824
Originally some distance from modern settlement. Moved bodily in 1952/3 but some parts confused in rebuilding. Trans. north doorway, some windows, lower part of tower and possible font. Rest is Perp.

FEWSTON ST LAWRENCE   WR (NY) SE 1954
Perp. tower with top added in 1697 when church was rebuilt. Nave and aisle under one roof (a Yorkshire fashion?). Medieval font with 'Jacobean' cover.

FILEY ST OSWALD   ER (NY) TA 1180
Cruciform and finest church in area. Mainly EE but some Trans.

work. Chancel, unusually lower than nave, has good EE sedilia. Small thirteenth-century effigy of priest, probably commemorating heart burial. Medieval bench end in south porch. Reredos of 1911.

FINGHALL   ST ANDREW   NR (NY) SE 1889
Remote Trans. church. Dec. east and south windows. Ninth-century crucifix built into chancel wall (other A/S fragments). Unusual coffin lid, bits of medieval glass, pulpit of mid-seventeenth century.

FISHLAKE   ST CUTHBERT   WR (SY) SE 6513
Impressive Perp. but its gem is the Norman south doorway, perhaps the most lavishly decorated in the county. Priest's doorway is also Norman. EE work in lower tower and handsome nave arcades. Extensive Dec., especially east window. Perp. clerestory, several windows, upper stage of tower (with niche and statue), battlements and pinnacles, parclose screens and font (Jacobean cover). Impressive tomb-chest (1505) which (not surprisingly) has lost its brass effigy.

FLAMBOROUGH   ST OSWALD   ER (H) TA 2270
Nineteenth-century tower, chancel and south aisle. Norman font and chancel-arch. Chapels Perp. (rebuilt in nineteenth century). Chancel-screen Perp. and best in ER. Early sixteenth-century Constable monument with long verse inscription.

FOLKTON   ST JOHN EVANGELIST   ER (NY) TA 0574
Norman nave, chancel and (blocked) north doorway; EE tower, Perp. windows in nave. Some A/S stones built into tower, Norman font, fragments of fourteenth-century glass in a north window, early twentieth-century glass in east window.

FORCETT   ST CUTHBERT   NR (NY) NZ 1712
Norman south doorway, tower and (reused) south porch entry. Rest mostly from drastic restoration of 1859 which also produced complete refurnishing in sumptuous High Victorian manner. Many sculptural fragments: A/D and medieval coffin lids. Worn effigy of fourteenth-century priest, allegorical monument of 1637.

FORDON   ST JAMES   ER (H) TA 0575
Small Norman church in delightful situation. Much restored in

eighteenth century and later. Norman doorway and reused fragments. Trans. font.

FOSTON ALL SAINTS   NR (NY) SE 6965

Unsympathetically developed in 1911 (north aisle, south porch and bell-cote) but retains treasures, especially remarkable south doorway. Norman pillar piscina, mysterious aumbry, eighteenth-century pulpit and panelling from recycled box-pews. Modern reading-desk in pelican form. Eighteenth-century hat pegs. Wall plaque to Sydney Smith (incumbent 1806–29) who designed rectory.

FOSTON-ON-THE-WOLDS ST ANDREW   ER (H) TA 1055

Norman nave and chancel, thirteenth-century south arcade, windows and sedilia (cut into by one of several Perp. windows). Dec. tower. Bits of medieval glass, defaced fourteenth-century effigy. Curious plastering (of the twentieth century) inside tower.

FRICKLEY ALL SAINTS   WR (SY) SE 4608

Small, lonely church, originally Norman (chancel-arch). Much late thirteenth-century work (north arcade, tower) with Perp. modifications. Substantial rebuilding in 1875 (especially south side). Restoration in 1930s by Comper (east window, pulpit, altar, organ case).

FRIDAYTHORPE ST MARY   ER (H) SE 8759

Norman work of *c.* 1140 ('barbaric' south doorway, chancel, font) and *c.* 1190 (fine tower). Thirteenth-century north arcade and chancel lancets. Modifications in seventeenth and eighteenth centuries, restoration in 1903 produced north aisle and south porch. Twelfth-century sculpture at apex of chancel-arch. Coffin lids.

FYLINGDALES: *see* ROBIN HOODS BAY

GANTON ST NICHOLAS   ER (NY) SE 9877

Mostly early Perp. (that is, late fourteenth century): tower, porch, good doorway, north aisle and windows. Chancel-arch may date from thirteenth century. South door has medieval hinges. South transept appropriated as Legard Mausoleum; Fisher monuments in chancel and north aisle.

GARTON ST MICHAEL   ER (H) TA 2365
Roughly built of cobble in thirteenth century. Font may be of this date or a century or more later. Much restored Perp. screen. Number of grotesque heads on chancel corbels and good top on churchyard cross.

GARTON-ON-THE-WOLDS ST MICHAEL   ER (H) SE 5859
Fine Norman church established by Kirkham Priory in 1132. Dec. window, Perp. modifications to tower. Later nineteenth-century restoration by Street includes remarkable frescoes, tile-work, mosaic pavement, painted roofs, reredos, pulpit. Worn Norman sculpture over west door, fourteenth-century effigies in tower.

GATE HELMSLEY ST MARY   NR (NY) SE 6955
EE arcades and reused window, Perp. tower. Substantially rebuilt in 1856. Porch has interesting Norman stoup. Wall tablets.

GIGGLESWICK ST ALKELDA   WR (NY) SD 8163
Completely rebuilt in Perp. period. Chancel slightly lower than nave. Handsome later seventeenth-century woodwork includes pulpit, reading-desk, communion rail. Poor-box of 1684, early eighteenth-century candelabra. Three defaced effigies. Royal Arms (1716, that is, George I). North aisle chantry chapel was original Giggleswick school (1488+) for local children. Monument to George Birkbeck, originator of Mechanics' Institute. St Alkelda is entirely unknown apart from two Yorkshire titles. She is said to have been an A/S maiden slaughtered by pagan Danes in the tenth century.

GILLING (EAST) HOLY CROSS   NR (NY) SE 6176
Arcades of *c.* 1200, chancel Dec., tower possibly dates from late sixteenth century. Sculptural fragment (possibly tenth century) under tower, very interesting fourteenth-century monumental slab. Late sixteenth-century effigies of Fairfax and wives and early nineteenth-century memorial to a later Fairfax couple.

GILLING (WEST) ST AGATHA   NR (NY) NZ 1805
Norman tower and (lost) north chapel, Dec. arcades and two-storeyed vestry. Much alteration in 1845 included additional north aisle, distorting shape of church. EE font, A/S fragments in porch.

Interesting Boynton monument of 1531 and two early eighteenth-century tablets.

GISBURN   ST MARY   WR (L) SD 8248
Mostly Perp. but tower is largely Norman and there is a good deal of
EE work including doorway, some windows and arches. Perp. screens
and some fifteenth-century glass.

GOLDSBOROUGH   ST MARY   WR (NY) SE 3856
Norman doorway. Mostly late thirteenth century (fine east window
and porch entrance) and after (Dec. south arcade tomb recess, later
north arcade, Perp. tower top). Effigies of knights, one especially
good. Fine eighteenth-century monument to Byerleys. Rare
seventeenth-century glass. Mass dial.

GOODMANHAM   ALL SAINTS   ER (H) SE 8842
Supposed to occupy site of heathen temple destroyed in 627 by its
converted chief priest, Coifi. Much Norman work and Trans. north
aisle, tower heightened in EE period and nave windows inserted in
Dec. Perp. clerestory and roof. Remarkable inscribed font (c. 1530)
with richest decoration in ER. Interesting monumental slab showing
only bust and feet.

GOXHILL   ST GILES   ER (H) TA 1844
Though built in 1840, retains items of interest. Norman font with
Tree of Life, excellent Perp. piscina, unusual monument to Johanna
de Lilley (probably of the early fourteenth century).

GREAT AYTON   ALL SAINTS   NR (NY) NZ 5510
A good deal of Norman work in both nave and chancel, though
windows are mainly of 1790. Tower demolished 1880. Two A/S
cross-heads. Three-decker pulpit. Churchyard contains graves of
members of Captain Cook's family and many well-carved headstones.

GREAT DRIFFIELD   ALL SAINTS   ER (H) TA 0257
Magnificent Perp. tower, containing reused A/S material (invisible).
Restoration and rebuilding in 1880 included north aisle and chapel
but much early thirteenth-century work survives in south doorway,
font, arcades and clerestory. Fourteenth-century south aisle

windows. Fine architectural fragments of twelfth to thirteenth century. Thirteenth-century bishop (Paulinus?) outside on east side. Figures from early seventeenth-century monument, early eighteenth-century chandelier, early twentieth-century screens by Temple Moore.

(GREAT) EDSTONE   ST MICHAEL   NR (NY) SE 7084
EE nave, eighteenth-century chancel, bell-turret. A/D sundial inscribed 'Time-teller for wayfarers. Othan wrought me'. Norman font. Seventeenth-century communion rail.

GREAT GIVENDALE   ST ETHELBURGA?   ER (H) SE 8153
Delightful situation. Rebuilt 1849 but reusing old material: Norman chancel-arch, low side and other windows of thirteenth-century. Stoup of same date preserved. Late eighteenth-century monument.

GREAT LANGTON   ST WILFRID   NR (NY) SE 2996
Roughcast building of simple Norman plan. Priest's doorway inserted in Dec. period, together with fine east window. Early fifteenth-century effigy of priest.

GREAT OUSEBURN   ST MARY   WR (NY) SE 4461
Norman tower with EE bell-openings. EE arcade, Perp. chancel. Nineteenth-century rebuilding of aisles (1820) and north chapel added in 1883.

GREAT SMEATON   ST ELOY   NR (NY) NZ 3404
Unique title of church now consisting mostly of undistinguished 1862 work. However, there is a Norman font and a south arcade of *c.* 1400. St Eloy was a French missionary-bishop (*d. c.* 658). He was regarded as the patron of goldsmiths (among others).

GRINTON   ST ANDREW   NR (NY) SE 0498
Strong Perp. impression but there are earlier remains including Norman tower, parts of nave which antedate tower, font. There are bits of EE, and south arcade may be Dec. Perp. parclose screens, font cover, and fragments of glass; seventeenth-century pulpit with later tester (1718); seventeenth- and eighteenth-century memorials. Possible evidence of anchorage.

GUISBOROUGH   ST NICHOLAS   NR (Cl) NZ 6115
Originated as chapel provided by nearby Austin priory. Rebuilt
c. 1500 with further modification in eighteenth and early twentieth-
centuries. Fragments of original glass in south aisle. Early twentieth-
century reredos. Treasure is outstanding Brus cenotaph (c. 1530)
removed from priory at its dissolution (rebus of James Cockerell, prior
1519–34).

GUISELEY   ST OSWALD   WR (WY) SE 1941
Norman work in south doorway and south arcade. Fine EE south
transept. Perp. north arcade and tower. Church greatly extended and
modified in early twentieth century. Some original Jacobean work
convincingly imitated in Nicholson's refurbishing. A/S fragments,
rood-beam of 1921.

HACKNESS   ST PETER   NR (NY) SE 9690
A/S chancel-arch, Norman south arcade, north arcade c. 1200, EE tower
with spire and battlements of fifteenth century together with clerestory.
Vestry sixteenth century or later. Important A/S cross from nunnery
founded in seventh century. Perp. font cover and stalls with misericords,
Jacobean pulpit, fine seventeenth-century candle-sticks (from Spain?).
Sixteenth-, seventeenth- and nineteenth-century monuments.

HALIFAX   ST JOHN   WR (WY) SE 0825
One of largest parish churches in WR. Mainly fifteenth-century Perp.
but some Norman and EE. Fine ceilings of early seventeenth century.
Excellent Perp. font cover and stalls used as sedilia ('brought in').
Outstanding communion rail (1698), box pews of half-century earlier,
remarkable poor-box ('Old Tristram'), probably of seventeenth
century in spite of inscribed date. Decorative leading in aisle windows
of Cromwellian period. Many monuments. Organ case from Scott's
restoration of 1879.

HALSHAM   ALL SAINTS   ER (H) TQ 5909
Much Perp. work (tower, windows, south arcade) but also some
Norman and Trans. pieces (sedile, for example, cut into by
magnificent Dec. sedilia and piscina). South aisle Dec., north chapel
largely eighteenth century. Pulpit (1634). Alabaster tomb-chest with
good effigy (later fifteenth century).

HAMPSTHWAITE   ST THOMAS BECKET   WR (NY) SE 2558
Rebuilt 1902 but Perp. tower survives. Remarkable collection of
coffin lids built into porch. Mutilated small brass of civilian *c.* 1380.
Extravagant marble monument to popular composer, Amy
Woodforde-Finden, †1919. Strong box. Rare surviving title.

HAREWOOD   ALL SAINTS (R)   WR (WY) SE 3245
In spite of some eighteenth-century work and restoration of 1863,
church is essentially Perp. Its treasure is the remarkable set of
recently restored monuments: six medieval ones of alabaster effigies
on tomb-chests and one of eighteenth century. Very interesting
details. Perhaps best is Judge Gascoigne (+1419). Thirteenth-
century font.

HARPHAM   ST JOHN OF BEVERLEY   ER (H) TA 0961
Norman and Dec. windows. Tower *c.* 1300. North chapel and aisle
Dec. Chancel repaired in brick (1827?) and east window made
c. 1910. Monuments include best brass in Riding (1418), fine
alabaster tomb-chest with incised effigies (1349+), very good (1762)
memorial to Charlotte St Quintin. Eighteenth-century armorial
glass by Peckitt. (Eighth-century St John of Beverley was born in
Harpham.)

HARROGATE   ST WILFRID   WR (NY) SE 3055
The finest church in Harrogate, built between 1905 and 1935, a nice
combination of modernity and tradition, fashion and originality.
Good furnishings and glass.

HARTHILL   ALL HALLOWS   WR (SY) SP 3293
Trans. arcades; EE chancel; Dec. east window; Perp. tower, south
chapel, clerestory; Victorian windows. Chapel screens are recycled
gates (sixteenth to seventeenth century), unusual Jacobean font cover,
eighteenth-century communion rail. Some Italian glass of 1884.
Seventeenth- and eighteenth-century monuments.

HARTSHEAD   ST PETER   WR (WY) SE 1622
Mainly Victorian 'Norman' of 1881 (some seventy years after P.
Bronte's incumbency). Genuine Norman work in tower, south porch
and chancel-arch. Old parish school in churchyard.

HATFIELD ST LAWRENCE   WR (SY) SE 6609
Large cruciform church with proud crossing-tower (early sixteenth
century with Savage heraldry). Much Norman work, thirteenth-
century arcades, some Dec., more Perp., windows including fine
clerestory. Further Perp. work in north and south chapels (which
retain original ceilings) and impressive east front. Font of *c*. 1300 with
nineteenth-century bowl. Good Perp. chancel-screen. Medieval,
seventeenth- and eighteenth-century monuments. Two parish chests
(possibly medieval).

HAUXWELL ST OSWALD   NR (NY) SE 1693
Eleventh-century herring-bone and chancel-arch, later Norman
south doorway (with tympanum) and nearby window. Tower *c*. 1200
(top *c*. 1600), EE chancel, fourteenth-century north chapel. Font is
'construct' utilizing base of thirteenth-century pier. Two late medieval
stalls, Jacobean pulpit and reading-desks. Monuments from fourteenth
to eighteenth centuries. Churchyard has A/D cross (originally with
Latin inscription saying it was 'Cross of St James'), also ejected font
(possibly eighteenth century).

HAWNBY ALL SAINTS   NR (NY) SE 5389
Basically Norman, now away from village. Much altered in fourteenth
to fifteenth century. Mysterious Latin cross with holes and incised
lines, said to be Norman. Seventeenth-century Tankard monuments.

HAWORTH ST MICHAEL   WR (WY) SE 0337
Rebuilt 1880, leaving only tower (possibly eighteenth century) of
church known to Brontes who are commemorated in chapel
(refurbished 1964) which contains some furniture from earlier church.

HAYTON ST MARTIN   ER (H) SE 8145
Masonry from all medieval periods. Perp. tower top is of unusual
design. Nave and chancel retain ancient roofs. Woodwork from Perp.
screen incorporated in stalls. East window has sixteenth-century glass
which may be Flemish.

HEALAUGH ST JOHN   WR (NY) SE 4947
Built *c*. 1130–50 with memorable south doorway. North aisle and
priest's doorway about forty years later. South door is Perp.

woodwork (probably fifteenth century), pulpit reuses some Jacobean material. North chapel with imposing monument to Thomas Lord Wharton (†1568) and two wives.

HEDON ST AUGUSTINE   ER (H) TA 1828
Though much reduced, still one of grandest ER churches. Much EE work, supplemented by Perp., including crossing-tower which rises to 128 ft (42 m). South transept built 1868. Two-storeyed sacristy on south side. Dec. font. Imposing thirteenth-century grave slab in black marble, late fourteenth-century bearded effigy, good tablet of 1721. Royal Arms of 1585.

HELMSLEY ALL SAINTS   WR (NY) SE 6183
Built 1869 in 'EE' style but reuses Norman doorway and chancel-arch, together with a good deal of EE work. Pretty piscina (Perp.) in north aisle, worn late fifteenth-century brass, fine Baroque chandelier. Altar and aisle roof by Temple Moor (c. 1910), font cover by Pace (1960s?). Tenth-century hog-back monument.

HEMINGBROUGH ST MARY   ER (NY) SE 6730
Appropriated to Durham Abbey, made collegiate in 1426. Most noticeable architectural feature is high, slim spire (early fifteenth century) rising from low tower of thirteenth century (time of major building activity). Perp. north chapel and many windows. Priest's doorway of south chapel worth close examination (c. 1500?). Font (c. 1200), Perp. screens. Eliz. fragments of another. 'Jacobean' pulpit (dated 1717!). Misericord of c. 1200. Most complete set of bench ends in ER. Fifteenth-century stone table. Cadaver (c. 1500) and unusual wooden memorials of seventeenth and eighteenth centuries.

HESSLE ALL SAINTS   ER (H) TA 0326
Chancel and east part of nave carefully rebuilt in 1870 but much untouched EE and Perp. work, as well as Dec. north aisle windows. Rare medieval paintwork on capitals. Some good Victorian glass.

HICKLETON ST WILFRID   WR (SY) SE 4805
Essentially Perp. but retains Norman chancel-arch. Lavishly provided with much 'brought in' furniture (Pevsner thinks that even font is recycled). Good churchyard cross and lych-gate with *memento mori*.

Perp. parclose screen, medieval pulpit (probably French), German statues and reliefs of sixteenth and eighteenth centuries and others of unknown provenance, Italian painting (c. 1500), eighteenth-century candelabra, Halifax memorials, bust of G.F. Bodley, church architect.

HIGH MELTON   ST JAMES   WR (SY) SE 5001
Norman chancel-arch, south arcade; Dec. doorways; rest (including tower) Perp. (note shields below east window exterior). Perp. parclose screen, fifteenth-century glass in chancel and south aisle which also has heraldic glass of eighteenth and early nineteenth centuries. Comper reredos and rood-screen (1927). Good Fountayne tablet (+1780).

HILTON   ST PETER   NR (Cl) NZ 4611
Small Norman church with primitive bell-cote and windows of seventeenth or eighteenth century. Neither east nor west windows. Unbonded Norman east wall indicates abandonment of original apse plan. Fine Norman relief reset in south wall. Primitive eighteenth-century font.

HINDERWELL   ST HILDA   NR (NY) NZ 7916
Norman (or earlier) origin but rebuilt in 1774 and tower added in 1817. Remnant of Norman pillar piscina in chancel. In north part of churchyard, remains of holy well of St Hilda (place-name means 'Hild's Spring').

HOLME-ON-SPALDING-MOOR   ER (H) SE 8138

ALL SAINTS
Standing lonely on its hill with 'one of the best churchyards in ER' (Pevsner), the church has fine Perp. tower with seated figure in a niche. Inside there are EE arcades, Dec. and Perp. windows, and clerestory and nave roof of latter period. There is patching (probably seventeenth century) and eighteenth-century porch. Restoration c. 1910. Perp. parclose screen and recycled fragments in stalls, seventeenth-century pulpit with tester, west gallery of 1767, early nineteenth-century box pews.

HOOTON PAGNELL   ALL SAINTS   WR (SY) SE 4808
Neighbouring the hall with its fourteenth-century gatehouse, the church is basically early Norman with north aisle added in Trans.

period, chancel extended in thirteenth century, tower modifed in early fourteenth and whole restored in 1876. Door hinges probably *c.* 1100. Eighteenth-century pulpit with marquetry.

HOOTON ROBERTS ST JOHN BAPTIST WR (SY) SK 4897
In spite of extensive rebuilding after disastrous fire, *c.* 1700, the small church retains a Trans. arch (probably from original chancel). Medieval modifications added two chapels, Perp. tower and battlements. Fragments of thirteenth-century glass. Church said to be burial place of Earl of Strafford (executed 1641).

HORBURY ST PETER AND ST LEONARD WR (WY) SE 2918
John Carr, born in the village in 1723, provided this church at his own expense (1793) and is buried in the crypt. It is a fine example of his work and contains some family monuments. Contemporary pulpit and brass to vicar (1834–99).

HORNBY ST MARY NR (NY) SE 2293
Large church with eleventh-century tower (Perp. top). Trans. north arcade but dominantly Dec. with early fifteenth-century south arcade. (Some Victorian work of 1877.) Good eighteenth-century font in Dec. style. Much restored Perp. screen with rare original painting. Fragments of late medieval glass. Monuments include stone and alabaster effigies (fourteenth century), brass (1489+), wall monument (1578) and tablet (1780).

HORNSEA ST NICHOLAS ER (H) TA 2047
A thirteenth-century church, enlarged and elaborated in the fourteenth and fifteenth centuries to produce very impressive interior. The thirteenth-century tower (heightened in Perp. period) is embraced by aisles. There are chancel chapels (one has gone), many Perp. windows (especially in bright chancel), and a small crypt of two chambers (one with fireplace!). Thirteenth-century font. Three monuments with effigies (fourteenth century) and alabaster tomb-chest (1430+).

HORTON-IN-RIBBLESDALE ST OSWALD WR (NY) SD 8172
Everything under one roof (except Perp. tower) in a Yorkshire fashion. Norman south door, some arcades and font. Perp. work in aisles and their windows. Fragments of medieval glass. Two lych-gates.

HOTHAM   ST OSWALD   ER (H) SE 8934
Exterior largely dates from 1905 restoration but short, broad tower is
Norman and there is an EE window in nave which has a brick
building to north, built in early nineteenth century to accommodate
squire's pew. Medieval glass fragments. Much modern glass-work by
Strachan (*d*. 1950).

HOVINGHAM   ALL SAINTS   WR (NY) SE 6675
Rebuilt 1860 except for A/S tower with (replaced) pyramidical roof.
Chancel retains one Norman and one EE (low side) window. Treasure
is carved A/S slab (altar frontal?) of *c*. 800, other and later A/S
fragments. Worsley monuments and seventeenth- and eighteenth-
century tablets.

HOWDEN   ST PETER   WR (H) SE 7428
Magnificent cruciform church, crowned with grand tower at crossing.
Formerly collegiate, dissolved at Reformation resulting in subsequent
decay (quire collapsed in 1696 and chapter-house in 1750). Built in
thirteenth and fourteenth centuries (note especially EE porch, Dec.
nave and fine west front). Tower completed early fifteenth century
with other Perp. additions. Grammar school attached to south aisle
c. 1500. Parts of gorgeous pulpitum recycled as reredos and aisle
screens. Dec. font. Ancient bits of glass in south porch and complete
modern windows in north transept (Stammers, 1953). Fine
fourteenth-century effigies, fifteenth-century brass, incised slab of
1513+, ledger stone by E. Gill in chapter-house (1913+). Church also
contains old parish coffin and a plough.

HUBBERHOLME   ST MICHAEL   WR (NY) SD 9178
Norman tower, nave and aisles under one roof (possibly fifteenth
century) in Yorkshire manner. Remarkably rough interior difficult to
date. Font inscribed 1696 but probably Perp. Treasure is chancel
screen, complete with loft built in 1558. Modern woodwork by
Thompson of Kilburn. Pretty window of 1970.

HUDDERSFIELD   ST PETER   WR (WY) SE 1416
Norman foundation but rebuilt in 1836. Rare font of 1570 with
Royal Arms of Elizabeth I. Unusual altar canopy (1921) by Comper
(east window glass by same artist).

HUGGATE ST MARY   ER (H) SE 8855
Norman work in chancel-arch and elsewhere; Trans. arcades. Tower and spire of fourteenth century and Perp. clerestory. Font of latter period.

HULL HOLY TRINITY   ER (H) TA 0929
Originating as thirteenth-century chapel-of-ease for new town. Rebuilding on grand scale began in early fourteenth century (transepts), followed by chancel (c. mid-fourteenth century), nave (c. 1400), tower (c. 1500) to produce largest parish church in England. Brickwork some of earliest in country. Fine Dec. font (and door to rood loft). Some quire stalls of same period or later. Perp. parclose screens, communion table of 1750 (in retroquire), nave furnishings of earlier nineteenth century. Numerous monuments include de la Poles (south quire aisle), late fourteenth-century effigy (south transept). Glass by Crane (c. 1900) in nave.

ST MARY LOWGATE
Chapel-of-ease to North Ferriby until 1661. Built throughout fifteenth century (tower rebuilt 1697). Over-restored in nineteenth century. Some medieval heraldic glass, fine plate brass of 1526 (John Haryson).

HUMBLETON SS PETER AND PAUL   ER (H) TA 2234
EE chancel and south arcade; Perp. north arcade, south doorway, tower (with interesting stair-turret). South door is Perp. and has ogee-headed wicket. Eighteenth-century work in one window and porch.

HUNMANBY ALL SAINTS   ER (NY) TA 0977
Mainly Norman; EE and Perp. bays in arcade. Perp. tower top, possible seventeenth-century porch. Restoration of 1845 produced much of woodwork. Two good eighteenth-century monuments (Osbaldeston, Staveley).

HUNTINGTON ALL SAINTS   NR (NY) SE 6156
1874 reusing old material (twelfth-century south doorway, EE pier, Perp. work in chancel). Inscribed Jacobean pulpit. Vicarage of 1903.

HUSTHWAITE ST NICHOLAS   NR (NY) SE 5175
Much Norman work includes doorways, chancel-arch, lower tower

(Perp. top). 1895 restoration inserted 'Norman' windows in nave. Seventeenth-century furniture: canopied pulpit, communion rails, pews and font cover.

HUTTON BUSCEL   ST MATTHEW   NR (NY) SE 9784
Norman tower with EE modifications. Restored north aisle retains EE work. Perp. south aisle, clerestory and south porch (which contains some Norman work). Jacobean elements in pulpit. Eighteenth-century monuments and tablet. Good lych-gate.

HUTTON CRANSWICK   ST PETER   ER (H) TA 0253
Norman fragment in south doorway, EE arcades, Perp. tower, Victorian windows. Damaged thirteenth-century effigy. Good nineteenth-century tablets.

HUTTON RUDBY   ALL SAINTS   NR (NY) NZ 4606
EE chancel, Dec. south arcade, Perp. porch tower and nave extension. Fine Eliz. pulpit (c. 1590). Seventeenth-century pews. Early fourteenth-century effigy of priest. Lynley monuments. Eighteenth-century tablets. Bassoon from nineteenth-century church orchestra.

ILKLEY   ALL SAINTS   WR (WY) SE 1147
Largely rebuilt in 1860 but preserves thirteenth-century doorway and fifteenth-century tower. Substantial remains of important A/S crosses and mutilated Roman altars used to build A/S church. Good fourteenth-century effigy in recess. Jacobean font cover and family pew.

INGLEBY ARNCLIFFE   ALL SAINTS   NR (NY) NZ 4400
Rebuilt 1821 (to be away from village?). Reused Norman doorway and transferred effigies of c. 1330, notable for armour. Characteristic 'Gothic' glazing bars, contemporary pews and three-decker pulpit. Two sets of Royal Arms. Glass fragments allegedly from Mount Grace. Model sailing-ship hangs from roof. Original Norman font now at Newton-in-Cleveland.

INGLEBY GREENHOW   ST ANDREW   NR (NY) NZ 5806
Almost entirely rebuilt in 1741 but retains Norman chancel-arch and a window. Trans. north arcade and priest's doorway. Pier capitals are

puzzling (possibly nineteenth-century). Effigies: priest (thirteenth century), knight (possibly fourteenth century); both ill-preserved.

INGLETON ST MARY   WR (NY) NZ 9765
Rebuilt 1887, apart from Perp. tower. Contains one of finest Norman fonts in WR whose carvings include scenes from life of Christ.

KELLINGTON ST EDMUND   WR (NY) SE 5524
Norman traces but mainly EE (nave, chancel, lower tower) and Perp. (upper tower, north chapel, clerestory, porch). Nave roof has some original bosses. Font 1663. Large thirteenth-century grave slab ('serpent stone'). Gate-piers of churchyard allegedly of 1698. Edmund, the king of East Anglia who was martyred by heathen Danes in 870, gave his name to St Edmundsbury.

KEYINGHAM ST NICHOLAS   ER (H) TA 2425
Largely late thirteenth-century Perp. tower (once had spire) and brick clerestory. Thirteenth-century font. Rare hourglass stand by pulpit. Seventeenth-century monument.

KILBURN ST MARY   NR (NY) SE 5179
Two nineteenth-century restorations have left some Norman work in porch and part of chancel-arch. EE remains reused in east wall of vestry. Two interesting thirteenth-century coffin lids. Perp. tower. Seventeenth-century pews. Chapel refurnished in 1958 as a memorial to 'mouse man' (Thompson of Kilburn).

KILDWICK ST ANDREW   WR (WY) SE 0145
Very long low church under a single roof. Apart from four nave bays, Perp. (including screenwork in chancel, nave roof, font with Instruments of Passion). Jacobean pews, family pew (1633). A/S fragments, early fourteenth-century effigy and mid-eighteenth-century monument. Church possesses a cope made from Chinese royal garment. Churchyard has 'organ' gravestone.

KILHAM ALL SAINTS   ER (H) TA 0564
Good Norman doorway, other earlier remains built into big Perp. tower. Very fine thirteenth-century chancel with sedilia. Seventeenth-century porch. Eighteenth-century windows in nave. Norman font.

KILNWICK-ON-WOLDS   ALL SAINTS   ER (H) SE 9949

Heavily restored in 1871 but Norman north doorway and EE arcade survive. Good mid-seventeenth-century pulpit. 'Gothick' organ case (1836). Grimston monuments.

KILNWICK PERCY   ST HELEN   ER (H) SE 8249

In grounds of the 'big house'. Neo-Norman of 1865 but reuses some real work: north doorway and re-set south doorway, part of corbel-table. Much 'brought in' woodwork: seventeenth-century English, eighteenth-century Flemish.

KIPPAX   ST MARY   WR (WY) SE 4130

Largely Norman with 'herring-bone' everywhere. Early work of transitional A/S–Norman period. Thirteenth-century modifications include south doorway, (blocked) north doorway, and east window. Perp. tower top. A/S fragments of late tenth century. Font of 1663.

KIRBY GRINDALHYTHE   ST ANDREW   ER (NY) SE 9067

Built 1878 by G.E. Street who did much work in area for Sir Tatton Sykes. The masonry of the chancel was preserved as was the Norman tower which had been heightened and given a spire in fourteenth century. Most furnishing by Street apart from dominating mosaic on west wall. Thirteenth-century piscina and font (latter, disused, in tower). Commendable lych-gate.

KIRBY HILL (NR. BOROUGHBRIDGE)   NR (NY) SE 3865

ALL SAINTS

Small, remote and of pre-Conquest origin (possibly eighth century). Norman modifications included north aisle (now largely Victorian – as is tower) and north chapel. Chancel is fifteenth century. Many A/S fragments, some reused (even as gravestones). Medieval hinges to south door. Fifteenth-century bench ends. Traces of wall-painting.

KIRBY HILL (NR. RAVENSWORTH)   NR (NY) NZ 1306

ST PETER AND ST FELIX

Perp. impression strengthened by mighty tower but there is Norman work in chancel and EE in arcades and east window. Dakyn tablet of

1558 may be earliest signed monument in England. Good tablets of 1609 and 1821.

KIRBY MISPERTON   ST LAWRENCE   NR (NY) SE 7779
Fifteenth-century tower with nineteenth-century top. Chancel also of nineteenth-century but retains fifteenth-century vestry contemporary with south aisle. Some A/S stones inset in walls. Several eighteenth-century tablets.

KIRBY SIGSTON   ST LAWRENCE   NR (NY) SE 4194
Somewhat detached from village. Tower is eighteenth-century addition to substantially Norman church. Fourteenth-century arcade to north chancel chapel (with Danish-inspired carving on capitals). North aisle arcade is Trans. Font dated 1662, with contemporary communion rail. Early fourteenth-century effigy. Rood-screen by Temple Moore (c. 1895).

KIRBY UNDERDALE   ALL SAINTS   NR (NY) SE 8158
Interesting church in delightful setting. Early Norman (herring-bone) with tower and aisles a little later. EE south doorway and fourteenth-century window (north aisle). Much restored in 1871. Glass by Hardman (1871) in east window and Comper (1920) in south. Rood-beam and figures by Temple Moore (1887). Wilberfoss monument (1532) in porch. Roman (?) carving inset in north aisle wall.

KIRBY WISKE   ST JOHN BAPTIST   NR (NY) SE 3784
Reset Norman south doorway. Mostly Dec. Fine sedilia, piscina and Easter Sepulchre. Perp. tower. Large monument to Mrs Samuelson (1898).

KIRK BRAMWITH   ST MARY   WR (SY) SE 6111
Norman doorway and chancel-arch. Thirteenth-century tower arch, Dec. priest's doorway and nearby windows. Perp. tower top and east window. Modern nave ceiling by G. Pace, pews by Thompson of Kilburn. Much twentieth-century heraldic glass.

KIRKBURN   ST MARY   ER (H) SE 9858
Built 1139 whence nave survives with spectacular south doorway and barbaric font. EE and Perp. modifications to tower which has

remarkable staircase. Chancel rebuilt 1857 (screen and reredos by Street, c. 1872).

KIRKBURTON   ALL HALLOWS   WR (WY) SE 1912
Mainly of c. 1200 with a good deal of nineteenth-century work (north aisle, many windows and modifications to Perp. tower). Nave ceiling with bosses is Perp. as are many benches (others Eliz.). Fragments of A/S cross. Reset west door. Squint in north chancel wall believed to be from anchorage.

KIRKBY FLEETHAM   ST MARY   NR (NY) SE 2894
Norman south doorway and (blocked) north. EE south chapel and (vaulted) porch. Dec. north aisle. Perp. tower (with vaulted first stage). Nineteenth-century north arcade. Excellent fourteenth-century effigy. Eighteenth-century monuments include one by Flaxman.

KIRKBY MALHAM   ST MICHAEL   WR (NY) SE 8960
Entirely Perp. with characteristic silhouette of locality. Unusual feature of image-niches in nave piers. Norman font, Jacobean communion rail and family pews, later Georgian box pews, one sixteenth-century panel of German glass. Chancel woodwork of 1923. Early seventeenth-century vicarage. Stone stocks in churchyard.

KIRKBY MALZEARD   ST ANDREW   WR (NY) SE 2374
Badly damaged by fire in 1904 and largely rebuilt but fine Norman doorway survived as well as a good deal of EE work. Perp. tower with ornamented base. Fifteenth-century fragments of glass (vestry). Civilian brass of 1604.

KIRKBY MOORSIDE   ALL SAINTS   WR (NY) SE 6986
Tower largely eighteenth century, chancel nineteenth (but some material reused including fourteenth-century sedilia). EE nave arcades; strong two-storeyed Perp. porch (fifteenth century). Chancel-screen, altar and its rails by Temple Moore (1919). Side altar reredos has medieval panels, A/S and other stone fragments in vicarage porch.

KIRKBY OVERBLOW   ALL SAINTS   WR (NY) SE 3249
Nave rebuilt in 1780, tower the following year and whole 'restored' in

1872. Nevertheless, there is a (blocked) north doorway of an A/S date and a fine north transept of Dec. period. 1793 memorial in Coade stone.

KIRKBY WHARFE   ST JOHN   WR (NY) SE 5040
Entirely Victorian impression belied by Trans. south doorway and arcades. Chancel and some windows are EE and there is a good deal of Perp. work (including north chapel with 'brought in' screenwork). Many A/S cross fragments and bits of old glass from the fifteenth to seventeenth centuries. Woodwork of south door is seventeenth century.

KIRKDALE   ST GREGORY   NR (NY) SE 6787
Finely sited late A/S church with aisle added *c*. 1200, tower of 1827, and thirteenth-century chancel reconstituted in 1881. Feature is inscribed A/S sundial which tells of minster's complete rebuilding in 1060. Substantial A/S fragments (some from seventh century), fourteenth-century statue of Virgin, stone wall benches.

KIRK DEIGHTON   ALL SAINTS   WR (NY) SE 3950
Late Norman north doorway and arcade, south doorway and arcade of early fourteenth century. Dec. tower (with spire), Perp. clerestory, most aisle windows and battlements. Two Victorian restorations (one produced garish Minton tiles in sanctuary). Mid-seventeenth-century Burton memorial.

KIRK ELLA   ST ANDREW   ER (H) TA 0129
Fine EE chancel, arch and north arcade. South arcade probably Dec. Rare remains of Dec. screen under fine Perp. tower (built from 1450–4). Many monuments include spectacular Sykes (†1805). Fragments of former Norman doorway in churchyard.

KIRK HAMMERTON   ST JOHN BAPTIST   WR (NY) SE 4655
Church of 1891 using substantially complete A/S church as its south part. Saxon church consists of tower, nave and chancel. This church received Norman windows and a north aisle, *c*. 1200; Perp. window and interesting furnishings in what is now south chapel of Victorian church.

KIRKHEATON   ST JOHN   WR (WY) SE 1817
Rebuilt 1888 but conserves A/S fragments including stone with runic inscription, thirteenth-century coffin lid (and font?), Perp. north

chancel chapel (now full of Beaumont monuments) with eighteenth-century wooden lectern.

KIRKLEATHAM ST CUTHBERT NR (Cl) NZ 5921
Replaced by finely built church of 1763 (probably by Carr) attached to Turner mausoleum of 1740 (by Gibbs). Apart from spectacular fourteenth-century chest, furnishings largely eighteenth century: font, pulpit, reading-desk, communion table and rail. Possible thirteenth-century effigy, Coulthurst brass of 1631, many Turner monuments include small brass of 1628+.

KIRK LEVINGTON ST MARTIN NR (Cl) NZ 4309
Substantial restoration of 1883 but there is a Norman doorway and chancel-arch, and a largely EE chancel. Porch contains numerous pre-Conquest fragments, parts of a Norman tympanum and several unusually large coffin lids.

KIRKLINGTON ST MICHAEL NR (NY) SE 3181
EE chancel, some Dec. windows and doorways, other windows and tower Perp. Late fourteenth-century effigies in south aisle recesses (knight has no sword). Fragments of fifteenth-century glass, good pulpit of *c.* 1600 (said to be recycled four-poster from nearby hall). Tomb-chest with recumbent effigy (†1590).

KIRK SANDAL ST OSWALD (R) WR (SY) SE 6007
Somewhat remote from present village and looks Victorian but west wall is Saxon, south doorway and one window Norman. There are EE arcades, Dec. west window and late Perp. North chapel with much contemporary glass. Fine, but much restored, screens. Nineteenth-century south porch tower.

KIRK SMEATON ST PETER WR (NY) SE 5116
Much restored and somewhat rebuilt in 1864 but there are Trans. arches to chancel and tower (Perp. top). North arcade is thirteenth century, south rebuilt in nineteenth century. Norman font; Dec. sedilia, south doorway and one window.

KIRKTHORPE ST PETER WR (WY) SE 3520
Perp. throughout with west tower and north aisle. Jacobean poor-box,

font dated 1718. Some good eighteenth-century monuments. Churchyard contains graves of nun-refugees from French Revolution.

KNARESBOROUGH   ST JOHN   WR (NY) SE 3557
Trans. cruciform church rebuilt in fifteenth century when transepts were removed. Mostly Perp. but east parts retain EE features (especially south chapel with its sedilia, piscina, niches and tomb-recess). Perp. font with handsome cover of *c.* 1700. Poor-box (1600). fragmentary Jacobean parclose screen. Interesting Slingsby monuments. Morris glass. (Nearby are cliff chapel of Our Lady of the Crag and remains of St Robert's hermitage.)

LANGTOFT   ST PETER   ER (H) TA 0166
Thorough restoration, *c.* 1900, added north aisle but EE remains include tower, south porch and some of south arcade. The chancel is Dec. with fine sedilia. Perp. chancel-arch. The font (from deserted village of Cottam) is Norman with much barbaric carving and there are sculptural fragments from Norman period. Knowsley monument (†1774).

LANGTON   ST ANDREW   ER (H) SE 7967
Built in 1822, reusing some old material. Thirteenth-century font, Jacobean panelling in chancel, later seventeenth-century woodwork on north wall. Ingram monument of 1656+.

LASTINGHAM   ST MARY   NR (NY) SE 7290
Remarkable crypt (1078–85) of temporary Benedictine monastery. East end of church also from this period. Much EE work and Perp. tower. All well restored, *c.* 1880. Crypt contains many A/S fragments including remains of cross once 24 ft high. Hog-back and other A/D pieces. Two coffin lids. Parish bier.

LAUGHTON-EN-LE-MORTHEN   WR (SY) SE 5188

ALL SAINTS
Perp. tower with one of finest and most original spires in WR. Other Perp. work includes font, remains of stone chancel-screen and parclose, south arcade, east window and aisle windows with finely carved hood-moulds. Earlier work includes A/S north doorway with

inset Norman work (also some chancel windows, former priest's doorway and north arcade). EE chancel door and lancet.

LEAD   ST MARY (R)   WR (NY) SE 4636

Tiny, hall-like (18 ft long), alone in field. Village it once served said to have been destroyed in battle of Towton (1461). (Church may have lost its chancel at the same time.) Probably built in early fourteenth century, 'restored' in 1784 when it was crammed with pews to supplement older benches and provided with three-decker. Floor largely paved with medieval coffin lids.

LEAKE   ST MARY   NR (NY) SE 4390

Norman tower and north arcade (part); south aisle and chancel of *c.* 1300 (priest's door set in buttress). Perp. east window and clerestory. Pair of fine Perp. stalls from elsewhere (Bridlington priory?). Good Jacobean pews, substantial font cover (post-Restoration?). Part of former chancel-screen is reused in communion rails. Good Norman sculpture set in south wall of nave. Brass of *c.* 1530.

LEATHLEY   ST OSWALD   WR (NY) SE 2346

Early Norman tower added to earlier nave and chancel which were almost completely remodelled in late Perp. period. Capitals with Percy badge and Tudor rose. West door preserves elaborate twelfth-century ironwork.

LECONFIELD   ST CATHERINE   ER (H) TA 0143

Remains of A/S window (west wall). Mainly thirteenth century, with Dec. windows in aisles (Victorian in chancel). Brick tower and porch of seventeenth century. Jacobean pulpit. Several fragments of fourteenth- to fifteenth-century glass.

LEDSHAM   ALL SAINTS   WR (WY) SE 4529

Essentially Saxon (eighth century?). Tower raised in Norman period with further Perp. work (including spire). Perp. north aisle, porch and many windows. Restoration of 1871. Some fifteenth-century glass in south aisle window. Good seventeenth- and eighteenth-century monuments.

LEEDS   ST PETER   WR (WY) SE 3034

Medieval parish church replaced in 1841 with a significant building marking Anglican revival. Preserves spectacular A/S cross, fourteenth-century effigy, two fifteenth-century brasses and large number of later monuments. Fifteenth-century font with seventeenth-century cover. 'Brought in' medieval glass (east window) and much of nineteenth-century.

ST JOHN EVANGELIST, NEW BRIGGATE (R)
Extremely rare and very fine example of 1630s. Magnificent well-preserved interior with exceptionally rich woodwork.

HOLY TRINITY, BOAR LANE
Built 1727 with fine dignified interior of period. Impressive tower of 1839 in a Wrenish manner.

ST AIDAN, ROUNDHAY ROAD
Built 1894 in opulent basilican style (a very rare Victorian form). Brilliant Brangwyn mosaics (1916).

LEVEN   HOLY TRINITY   ER (H) TA 1045
Built 1844 to replace small medieval church on new site but preserves exceptionally fine churchyard cross-head of fifteenth century, some A/S fragments and thirteenth-century font.

LEVISHAM   ST MARY   NR (NY) SE 8390
Remote old church, restored in earlier nineteenth century and replaced by late nineteenth-century church in village. A/S chancel-arch and Norman work. A/D graveslab with dragon (c. 1000), eighteenth-century font (Norman font in 'new' church).

LINTON   ST MICHAEL   WR (NY) SE 9070
Well sited, attractive church. Basically Norman but considerably altered at beginning of fourteenth century and later. Norman font. Porch seats incorporate recycled window-heads. Unusual bell-turret.

LISSET   ST JAMES OF COMPOSTELLA   ER (H) TA 1458
Built 1876 but reused some Norman work from predecessor (doorway, capital set in wall, hog-back fragment). Good east window by Kempe (c. 1870?). Church said to possess oldest dated bell in England (1254).

LITTLE DRIFFIELD ST PETER   ER (H) TA 0157
Greatly (but carefully) restored by Temple Moore in 1889. Norman tower-arch and other incorporated medieval fragments. Detached fragments include remains of A/S cross-head etc. Eighteenth-century pulpit. Interesting tablet in chancel concerning Aldfrith who died in 705.

LITTLE OUSEBURN HOLY TRINITY   WR (NY) SE 4460
Norman tower and chancel windows (some thirteenth-century work) but mainly Perp. (tower top, nave, aisles, arcades, chancel-arch, east window). Three early sixteenth-century bench ends. Eighteenth-century Turner mausoleum in churchyard.

LIVERTON ST MICHAEL   NR (Cl) NZ 7116
Practically rebuilt 1903 but large chunks of Norman masonry survive as well as magnificent chancel-arch with its fascinating carving.

LOCKINGTON ST MARY   ER (H) SE 9947
Exterior of mixed brick and stone. Norman doorway and chancel-arch. Nave extended in thirteenth century and tower added. Dec. east window and low side windows (made by lengthening earlier ones). Perp. south arcade. Medieval glass fragments. Eighteenth-century pulpit and communion rail. Nineteenth-century west screen using earlier woodwork. South chapel reconstituted in 1635 as Estoft family monument with much heraldry. Moyser tomb, *c.* 1630.

LOCKTON ST GILES   NR (NY) SE 8489
Oldest parts seem EE but mainly Perp. impression (tower, east window). Main furniture provided in 1688: pulpit, reader's desk, communion rail.

LONDESBOROUGH ALL SAINTS   ER (H) SE 8645
Eleventh-century A/D cross-head inset above Norman doorway. Trans. priest's doorway and north arcade. EE north chapel, tower (with Perp. top) and unusual font. Early eighteenth-century pulpit. Rood-screen (and churchyard cross) by Temple Moore, *c.* 1885. Burlington monuments and banners.

LONG MARSTON ALL SAINTS   WR (NY) SE 4951
Late Norman work includes doorways, nave and chancel (two

windows survive), north arcade. Dec. east window, tower and other windows Perp. Unusual Thwaites monument of 1602, Calverley of 1740.

LONG PRESTON   ST MARY   WR (NY) SD 8357
Mostly Dec. with rebuilt chancel of 1868. Font of uncertain date (Norman?) but has 'Jacobean' cover dated 1726! Pulpit of earlier seventeenth century. Sundial (1659) in churchyard.

LOVERSALL   ST CATHERINE   WR (SY) SK 5798
Perp. (apart from lower tower) with restorations in 1850 and 1855. (South chapel late Perp. of *c.* 1530.) Fourteenth-century stalls, four with misericords. Early fourteenth-century effigy, tomb-chest (fifteenth century?) and eighteenth-century memorial. Most interesting monument is very rare (early fourteenth-century) example in churchyard.

LOW CATTON   ALL SAINTS   ER (H) SE 7053
Originally Norman cruciform church, modified in thirteenth century by north aisle and added porch, followed by south arcade and unusually placed south-west tower (Perp. top). Dec. work in north transept and several windows (others Perp.). Chancel largely 1866 work by Street. Thirteenth-century font. Good east window glass by Morris (1866).

LOWER BENTHAM   ST JOHN   WR (NY) SD 6407
Rebuilding, *c.* 1880, reused some old material (chancel and adjoining chapel arches, window-heads) and left Perp. tower. Possibly A/S crucifix. Medieval bell in porch.

LOWTHORPE   ST MARTIN   ER (H) TA 0860
Fine but ruined chancel of collegiate church, rest hacked about in eighteenth century. Victorian inserted windows and added porch. Doorway is EE and tower Perp. with later brick top. Remarkable (possibly unique) Heslerton monument of later fourteenth century. Brass of *c.* 1450.

LUND   ALL SAINTS   ER (H) SE 9748
Apart from Perp. tower, rebuilt in decade after 1845. Damaged

Norman font survives, also some interesting medieval monuments (also damaged).

LYTHE   ST OSWALD   NR (NY) NZ 8413
Somewhat isolated from present village on good site. Mostly rebuilt in 1910 but retains EE tower, Perp. north aisle and vestry. Attractive, well-furnished interior. Remarkable collection of fragments (mostly A/D of *c.* 1000). Mulgrave monuments.

MALTBY   ST BARTHOLOMEW   WR (SY) SK 3592
Rebuilding of 1859 spared the Norman tower to which another stage and spire had been added in Perp. period. A Norman font also survives.

MALTON   ST MICHAEL, NEW MALTON   NR (NY) SE 7871
Norman with Perp. tower, ruthlessly 'restored' in 1858 and 1883. Norman arcades in nave. Font probably seventeenth century in 'Norman' style. Modern woodwork. Many tablets.

ST LEONARD, NEW MALTON
Norman arcades and font. Perp. tower with small figure (St Leonard?) in relief on west face. Nineteenth-century spire. Iron monument to iron-founder (†1837). Rare example of medieval church restored to Catholic use.

ST MARY, OLD MALTON
Scanty remains of a former Gilbertine priory church. Fine façade of *c.* 1200 (inserted Perp. window). Fire of *c.* 1500 caused remodelling of west bays of nave (one pier has inscription relating to Prior Roger Bolton). Sparse furnishings include a few misericords. Organ case by Temple Moore (1888).

MANFIELD   ALL SAINTS   NR (NY) NZ 2213
Originally Norman but now mainly Victorian. Some original bits in priest's doorway, some EE windows and south arcade. North arcade, *c.* 1330. Impressive tower dates from somewhere between late Perp. and early eighteenth century. Ornate Victorian font.

MAPPLETON   ALL SAINTS   ER (H) TA 2244
Much Victorianized church, originally of Dec. and Perp. periods.

Dec. font, Perp. tower with Victorian spire. Brough monument of 1823.

MARKET WEIGHTON   ALL SAINTS   ER (H) SE 8741
Herring-bone masonry attests to early Norman origins. Much EE work: tower (with eighteenth-century brick top), chancel, north chapel, south door and porch. Dec. north arcade, Perp. south aisle and raised nave.

MARR   ST HELEN   WR (SY) SE 5105
Early Norman; chancel remodelled in thirteenth century and tower (with recessed spire) built c. 1300. Arcades of about same time and porch Perp. Font probably early fourteenth century. Rare sixteenth-century pulpit. Remains of medieval painting in south arcade. Funeral armour. Sixteenth-century brasses.

MARRICK   ST ANDREW   NR (NY) SE 0798
Built 1811 from recycled masonry of dissolved priory. Early nineteenth-century box pews, pulpit with Jacobean panels. Medieval glass fragments in original Perp. east window.

MARSKE   ST EDMUND   NR (NY) NZ 1000
Norman (south door, blocked north and possibly double bell-cote). Practically rebuilt in 1683 in medieval manner. Porch has mysterious sixteenth-century inscription. Font 1663. Two-decker pulpit, box pews and family pew of early nineteenth century.

MARTON-IN-THE-FOREST   ST MARY   NR (NY) SE 6068
Violent nineteenth-century restoration but cobble walls on north side and chancel-arch date from early Norman times. Short Perp. porch tower with canopied angel above doorway. Some rebuilding after dissolution of neighbouring Austin priory (1536) apparently cannibalizing material. A few pre-Reformation benches and woodwork of south door (c. 1500?). Medieval glass fragments in west window. Eliz. (?) altar rails.

MASHAM   ST MARY   NR (NY) SE 2280
Norman tower, raised and spire added c. 1400. Other Perp. modifications included clerestory and arcades. Victorian restoration,

especially of exterior. Fine, but much weathered A/S cross-shaft (ninth century) outside church (other fragments within). A north window has good glass by Stammers (1958). Painting in style of Reynolds (*c.* 1800) over chancel-arch. Many monuments include Wyvill (1613).

MELSONBY   ST JAMES   NR (NY) NZ 1908
Some Trans. work in arcades but church (including tower) is mainly EE (with Victorian restoration). Fine eighth-century fragments from A/S gravestones. Effigies include early fourteenth-century knight and an unusual civilian one (priest?) with head emerging from foliated cross.

METHLEY   ST OSWALD   WR (WY) SE 3826
A mixture of EE (windows), Dec. (windows and south arcade), and Perp. work (tower, porch, clerestory, fine roof and later south chapel (*c.* 1485). Heavy restoration in 1876. Chancel rebuilt 1926. Rich furniture and monuments include fine lectern (Flemish, *c.* 1500, modified when 'brought in' in 1869), font cover (1584+), late seventeenth-century screen, pulpit (1708). Excellent Waterton monuments in chantry chapel, other fifteenth-century memorials in alabaster and stone, also good examples from seventeenth, eighteenth and nineteenth centuries. Well-preserved fifteenth-century glass (Waterton chapel). Carving of St Oswald, by chancel-arch. Funeral armour.

MEXBOROUGH   ST JOHN   WR (WY) SK 4799
Away from present centre. Trans. north arcade, EE chancel and possibly original tower (Perp. modification including short spire). Late A/S cross-fragment. Interesting monuments.

MIDDLEHAM   ST MARY AND ST ALKELDA   NR (NY) SE 1287
Dec. work in chancel, arcades, south chapel and south doorway (with once fine carved crucifix). Perp. tower, clerestory and lofty font cover. A/S slab under tower, fine monument to Abbot Thornton (†*c.* 1333). Many fifteenth-century glass fragments (which include a portrayal of St Alkelda's martyrdom). Early Georgian Charity Boards. Memorial window (1934) to Richard III who made church collegiate in 1478 and whose son was born in neighbouring castle.

MIDDLETON ST ANDREW   NR (NY) SE 7885

A/S tower, heightened in thirteenth century when chancel was remodelled and new south aisle added. In between came the Trans. north arcade (c. 1140). Perp. clerestory, woodwork of south door and stalls (one with misericord). Eighteenth-century pulpit with attractive tester (porch may be of this century too). Restoration c. 1885 particularly affected chancel. Remarkable collection of sculptured fragments include substantial and interesting remains of three A/D crosses.

MIDDLETON-ON-THE-WOLDS   ER (H) SE 9449

ST ANDREW

Original masonry and fine early thirteenth-century chancel survive heavy restoration of 1874. Norman font, EE sedilia. The churchyard contains four (ejected and reused?) medieval tombstones.

MIDDLETON TYAS ST MICHAEL   NR (NY) NZ 2205

Exterior represents an EE church but inside there is evidence of both Norman and Dec. work. Chancel rebuilt and spire added in 1868. Monuments include magnificent thirteenth-century coffin lid (south aisle) and eighteenth-century wall tablet to Revd J. Mawer, which states that he was 'descended from king Coyl'.

MILLINGTON ST ETHELBURGA   ER (H) SE 8351

Norman nave, chancel and doorway. Porch and belfry in grey brick (possibly of eighteenth century). Pleasant country interior with west gallery. Eighteenth-century Frank monument.

(GREAT) MITTON ALL HALLOWS   WR (L) SD 7138

Nave and chancel built towards end of thirteenth century. Early fifteenth-century tower. Sherburne Chapel added 1594 as repository for family monuments. Excellent late Perp. rood-screen with reference to fifteenth-century abbot of Sawley (early nineteenth-century cast-iron cresting!), Sherburne Chapel screen may be recycled fifteenth-century material. Rare Eliz. font cover (1593) on Norman font; sixteenth- and seventeenth-century effigies; pulpit is a construct of late seventeenth century and early Georgian woodwork. Fourteenth-century cross-head restored to churchyard.

MONK FRYSTON ST WILFRID   WR (NY) SE 5029
A/S tower raised and strengthened in Perp. period. EE arcades,
chancel-arch (and probably font). Chancel Dec. Perp. clerestory and
aisle windows. Fragments of medieval glass, Jacobean communion rail,
reredos of 1909.

MOOR MONKTON ALL SAINTS   WR (NY) SE 5036
Apart from heavy restoration of 1879 (which also added tower),
mainly late Norman (doorways, for example). Defaced relief in
porch. Curious small monumental slab to priest (mid-fourteenth
century?).

MYTON-ON-SWALE ST MARY   NR (NY) SE 4366
Mainly thirteenth century but tower was inserted in 1887 (this, and
vestry, rather ruins line of arcades). Eighteenth-century glass depicting
Moses and Aaron (situated in north aisle, although difficult to see).
Kempe glass in chancel.

NAFFERTON ALL SAINTS   ER (H) TA 0559
Large, originally Norman (font, chancel-arch). Much Dec. work
(chancel, south aisle); Perp. tower, north aisle, clerestory. Seventeenth-
century nave roof. Box pews. East window (1854) signed by Wailes.
Some curious medieval monuments.

NETHER POPPLETON ST EVERILDA   WR (NY) SE 5654
Only nave and chancel survive of an originally cruciform Norman
church. Unusual west and north galleries of Georgian period.
Fragments of medieval glass. Seventeenth-century (Hutton)
monuments. Modern rood. Everilda was a seventh-century
aristocratic convert of St Birinus, the evangelist of Wessex and is said
to have moved north and founded a convent at Everingham.

NEW MALTON: *see* MALTON

NEWTON-IN-CLEVELAND ST OSWALD   NR (Cl) NZ 5713
A/S stone inset in south-east buttress of tower testifies to pre-
Norman church. Present one has Norman nave and chancel-arch.
Chancel (1857), tower (1901). Norman font (from Ingleby
Arncliffe).

NEWTON KYME ST ANDREW WR (NY) SE 4644

Small Perp. tower, many thirteenth- and fourteenth-century windows but one of Norman period survives in chancel. Some old heraldic glass. Scratched-in figures at porch entrance of uncertain date. Curious brick monument in churchyard (early twentieth century).

NORMANBY ST ANDREW NR (NY) SE 7381

A Norman church of which north arcade and some fragments survive. Remodelled in eighteenth century and 'restored' in 1895. Chancel-arch may have survived from c. 1300 but Perp. east window has been re-set in north wall. Rustic seventeenth-century communion rail and poor-box probably of same century.

NORMANTON ALL SAINTS WR (WY) SE 3822

Much discoloured by its industrial setting but a large church, much restored, mainly of Dec. and Perp. period. Fine font, perhaps mid-sixteenth century. Many fragments of medieval glass but none native to church. Fine south chancel chapel (c. 1500+). Good late sixteenth-century (Freeston) monument.

NORTHALLERTON ALL SAINTS NR (NY) SE 3794

Imposing church, largely Perp. in style with dominating crossing-tower. (Chancel is Victorian 'Perp.' of 1885.) There is a little Norman and considerable EE work (particularly in transepts). Font (1662) has contemporary cover. Many carved fragments of pre-Norman period and a king's head of later twelfth century.

NORTH CAVE ALL SAINTS ER (H) SE 8832

Large church built of rubble. Norman tower (with Perp. top) and much apparently thirteenth-century work. South porch dated 1753 and chancel was restored in early nineteenth century. Very curious transept which Pevsner suggests may be unique in its absence of north and south arches. Effigies of c. 1600. Twentieth-century east window (Strachan). Unique inscription on south wall of chancel.

NORTH DALTON ALL SAINTS ER (H) SE 9352

Norman doorway, chancel-arch. Chancel much restored with rest in 1872 (originally EE). Good Perp. tower with west window. East window designed by Burne-Jones (1877) but glass not entirely original.

NORTH FRODINGHAM   ST ELGIN   ER (H) TA 1053

Perp. tower with niche (top part of 1892). Church heavily restored 1878 but retains fine Perp. niche in north wall exterior and some EE and Dec. features inside. Good Flemish chest of *c.* 1530. A/S fragments. Title is puzzling as there is no record of a canonized Elgin.

NORTH GRIMSTON   ST NICHOLAS   ER (NY) SE 8467

Externally EE with eighteenth-century work in chancel. Norman chancel-arch and remarkable font with much primitive figure carving. Thirteenth-century statue of St Nicholas stands above west window (earlier panel over north door). Fine thirteenth-century coffin lid. Early seventeenth-century memorial and some tablets.

(NORTH) NEWBALD   ST NICHOLAS   ER (H) SE 9136

Most complete Norman church in ER (*c.* 1140). Central tower heightened in thirteenth century when EE windows were inserted. Perp. chancel. Trans. font (with a seventeenth-century cover). Thirteenth-century chest. Fine (but restored) Majestas over the south doorway.

NORTON, SHEFFIELD   ST JAMES   WR (SY) SK 3581

Restored Norman doorway, EE tower with additions in Perp. period which also recast church (exterior details, clerestory, etc.), finally south chancel chapel was built (*c.* 1520). Good EE font. Fine alabaster tomb-chest with Blythe effigies (*c.* 1515). Tablet to sculptor Chantrey who is buried in churchyard.

NUNBURNHOLME   ST JAMES   NR (H) SE 8548

Norman remains include chancel-arch recycled as tower-arch (tower 1901), windows include one EE, several Dec. Some fourteenth-century glass fragments. Remains of best A/S cross in ER (*c.* 1000).

NUN MONKTON   ST MARY   WR (NY) SE 5057

Surviving nave of church of Benedictine nunnery with magnificent Trans. and EE work. Wall dividing nave from destroyed chancel restored in 1873 and provided with window glass by Morris (finest in WR). Superb setting.

NUNNINGTON   NR (NY) SE 6679

ALL SAINTS AND ST JAMES
Seventeenth-century tower in Perp. style. Thirteenth-century church
(with modifications). A/S fragments. Fourteenth-century effigy.
Jacobean pulpit. EE font with eighteenth-century cover. Memorials
include Jackson (†1760) with interesting inscription. Unusual
combined title.

OLD BYLAND   ALL SAINTS   NR (NY) SE 5486
Unusually low porch-tower has an A/D inscribed sundial in east wall.
There are Norman fragments around porch (including panels with
dragons) and chancel-arch shows early Norman work. Interesting
tiling in sanctuary.

OLD MALTON: *see* MALTON

OSBALDWICK   ST THOMAS   NR (NY) SE 6351
Twelfth-century church, restored in 1877. A nave window of *c*. 1300
and simple Perp. east window. Jacobean pulpit and later seventeenth-
to eighteenth-century communion rail. Interesting inscription on
headstone (1645) by east wall of porch.

OSMOTHERLEY   ST PETER   NR (NY) SE 4597
On site of apsed A/S church. Norman south doorway and font,
chancel-arch probably EE (as is damaged piscina). Perp. tower and
window. South chapel of 1540+. Porch perhaps seventeenth century.
Much restored in 1892 (when south aisle was (re)built). Fragments
include A/D pieces.

OSWALDKIRK   ST OSWALD   NR (NY) SE 6279
A/S cross-shaft built into south-west corner of Norman nave
(doorway and one window). Some EE windows. A/S fragments in
porch and medieval glass in north window. Thirteenth-century coffin
lid with abbatial staff. Eighteenth-century tablets.

OTLEY   ALL SAINTS   WR (WY) SE 2045
Norman north doorway and windows in remarkably low chancel
which allows insertion of Dec. window in nave east wall. Other Dec.

and Perp. windows. Perp. arcade. Jacobean porch. Seventeenth- and eighteenth-century communion rails, eighteenth-century pulpit. Large and interesting collection of A/S fragments of ninth to eleventh centuries. Various monuments to important local families. In graveyard extension is noteworthy monument to men killed during making of Bramhope tunnel (1845–9).

OTTRINGHAM ST WILFRID   ER (H) TA 2624
Early Norman tower-arch, thirteenth-century lancet in chancel but mainly early fourteenth-century (Dec.), arcades and tower, for example. Perp. contribution included font, clerestory, nave roof with bosses, south door with ogee-headed wicket. Box pews, Victorian east window (glass by Stammers) and communion rail. Rare stone Gospel lectern in chancel.

OVER SILTON ST MARY   NR (NY) SE 4593
Norman (doorway, font) but with much Dec. and Perp. modification (especially windows). Damaged early sixteenth-century stall is part of fine set (others at Leake).

OWSTON ALL SAINTS   WR (SY) SE 5411
In former grounds of hall. Early Norman masonry, later tower heightened in EE period when north aisle was built. Dec. chancel and Perp. alterations to aisles and tower, with added south porch and North chapel. Fine Easter Sepulchre. Perp. screen. Brass (1417). Early nineteenth-century Chantrey monuments.

PANNAL ST ROBERT   WR (NY) SE 3051
Dec. chancel, Perp. tower, eighteenth-century nave (with nineteenth-century windows). Font, c. 1722. Many memorials to Bentley family who have been lay rectors since seventeenth century. Churchyard contains alleged mortsafe. The title commemorates famous early thirteenth-century hermit whose cell was at nearby Knaresborough.

PATRICK BROMPTON ST PATRICK   NR (NY) SE 2290
Trans. south doorway; Dec. chancel and south aisle. Tower rebuilt 1864. Fine Dec. sedilia, possible Easter Sepulchre. Holy water stoup from recycled Trans. pier. Eighteenth-century communion rail in south aisle. Fragments of medieval glass. Title here and at Patrington

commemorates some association of the 'apostle of Ireland' with these Yorkshire sites.

PATRINGTON   ST PATRICK   ER (H) TA 3622
One of finest parish churches in England, built almost entirely in the half century after 1300 (part of crossing-tower is EE). Dec. spire as elegant as any in country. Splendid Dec. sedilia, piscina, Easter Sepulchre and font. North and south porches. Fine architectural achievements include north transept door, south transept chapel, tower staircase. Thirteenth-century Virgin, late fifteenth-century screen, pulpit 1612, Jacobean benches in transept, colourful modern reredoses.

PAULL   ST MARY AND ST ANDREW   ER (H) TA 1626
Perp. cruciform church where ambition outstripped resources (short transepts, much rubble in walls). Some late medieval glass in east window. Gospel lectern in chancel wall. Unusual combined title.

PENISTONE   ST JOHN BAPTIST   WR (SY) SE 2402
Thirteenth-century nave arcades, Dec. chancel, South chapel and south doorway. Perp. period added fine tower, battlements, clerestory with pinnacles, chancel chapel, windows, good roof with bosses. Organ case by Pace (1975). Interesting Saunderson memorial.

PICKERING   SS PETER AND PAUL   NR (NY) SE 7983
Over-restored but contains material from all periods of medieval architecture (Norman crossing-arch, Trans. arcade, EE south transept, Dec. tower and chancel, Perp. porch, clerestory, battlements). A/D fragments, Dec. sedilia, eighteenth-century pulpit and chandeliers. Treasure is abundant survival of mid-fifteenth-century murals. Three effigies (1350–1400) and many tablets of eighteenth to nineteenth centuries.

PICKHILL   ALL SAINTS   NR (NY) SE 3483
Norman south doorway and chancel-arch, thirteenth-century north arcade and aisle, Dec. east window, late Perp. tower. Heavily restored 1877. Thirteenth-century monument. Font 1662. Fragment of screen (and part of seventeenth-century parclose reused in lych-gate). Pre-Conquest and later stone fragments.

POCKLINGTON   ALL SAINTS   ER (H) SE 8048
One of best Perp. towers in ER. Rest of church mainly late twelfth
and thirteenth centuries (apart from several Perp. windows and rebuilt
chancel). Curious projections from chancel-arch may have supported
backcloth to rood. Head of fine churchyard cross (with inscription
including 'Orate' and statement that St Paulinus preached here). Early
fourteenth-century stone table in sanctuary. Incised slab of 1512.
Wooden altarpiece (Flemish, c. 1520). Two late sixteenth-century
monuments. Organ case by Pace (1954).

PONTEFRACT   ALL SAINTS   WR (WY) SE 4522
Mainly of fourteenth and fifteenth centuries but badly damaged in
Civil War and lay in ruins until restoration of 1838. Further
restoration in 1967.

ST GILES
Former chapel-of-ease (c. 1300) raised to parochial status in 1789
when it was largely rebuilt. Chancel of 1869.

PRESTON   ALL SAINTS   ER (H) TA 1830
Fine tower emphasizes Perp. impression but there is EE work in north
arcade and Dec. in south. Perp. font. Substantial alabaster fragments of
reredoses and a length of (rood-?) beam with 'Orate'.

RASKELF   ST MARY   NR (NY) SE 4971
Extremely interesting church in spite of its modern appearance.
Fifteenth-century timber belfry (unique in county). Dec. south
doorway and nave. Norman north arcade. Nineteenth-century aisle.
Perp. north chapel with rare timber arcade. Rustic Perp. bench ends.
Nice font cover, parclose screen, communion rail of seventeenth
century. Medieval glass fragments.

RASTRICK   ST MATTHEW   WR (WY) SE 1321
Handsome building of 1798 with cupola on tower. Galleried interior
of period. Base of eleventh-century churchyard cross in cemetery
north-west of church.

REDMIRE   ST MARY   NR (NY) SE 0491
Some distance from present village. Small Norman church with rough

bell-cote and few windows. Fragment of Norman sculpture and part of early eighteenth-century staircase. EE font. Fragments of medieval glass. Corbels for rood-beam. Low side window. Scratch dial.

RICCALL   ST MARY   ER (NY) SE 6327
Fine Norman doorway with miniature carvings on capitals of colonnettes. Door and its ironwork contemporary. Porch of 1865 by Pearson who also carefully rebuilt tower. Early thirteenth-century arcades and later north chapel and chancel with nice piscina. Perp. south chapel, aisle windows and clerestory. Small room at west end of north aisle was probably an anchorage. Seventeenth-century communion rail and contemporary woodwork in bench and litany desk. Good tablet (Wormley 1711+).

RICHMOND   ST MARY   NR (NY) NZ 1701
Inconspicuously sited outside medieval town walls. Two nineteenth-century restorations have left Norman work in west arcade, EE in east arcade and also in north doorway. Dec. south doorway. Perp. north aisle, vaulted south porch and tower. Perp. font with Jacobean cover. Early sixteenth-century stalls with misericords and canopies (from Easby Abbey). Remains of fifteenth-century wall-paintings. Hutton monument of 1629 with interesting verse inscriptions.

RILLINGTON   ST ANDREW   ER (NY) SE 8574
Norman work in north chapel, some EE remains and Dec. chancel-arch. Perp. tower with modern spire. Restoration of 1885. Trans. font with seventeenth-century cover.

RIPLEY   ALL SAINTS   WR (NY) SE 2860
Rebuilt c. 1400 after landslide. Interesting tower completed in 1567 when clerestory was added. South chapel has domestic accommodation on upper floor. North arcade reuses thirteenth-century material, while south is Perp. (Heavy Perp. parclose screen to south chapel.) Fine Ingleby monument (1369+). Others of seventeenth century. Chalice brass (1429+). Base of 'weeping cross' in churchyard.

ROBIN HOOD'S BAY   ST STEPHEN (R)   NR (NY) NZ 9605
Parish church of Fylingdales. New church is big, stern work of 1870 by Street with very good contemporary glass by Holiday. The old

church is about a mile to the north-west and was built in 1822 on a very old site. It retains an unaltered interior, characteristic of its period, with galleries, box pews and a three-decker pulpit. Inside and out there are many memorials to the shipwrecked.

ROECLIFFE   ST MARY (R)   WR (NY) SE 3766
Small church of 1843 designed in the fashionable neo-Norman style by Yorkshire architect Richard H. Sharp. Impressive tunnel-vault overhangs remarkable collection of 'brought in' ecclesiastical furniture among tiers of pews ranged along north and south walls.

ROMALDKIRK   ST ROMALD   NR (D) NY 9921
Cruciform church of late twelfth century with subsequent modifications in all Gothic periods (EE windows in south aisle and south transept; Dec. in north transept and chancel; Perp. east window and tower. Norman font. Dec. double piscina. Interesting north annexe to chancel, of two storeys with grilled upper window and squint (not towards high altar). Fine effigy of 1304+. Early eighteenth-century pulpit (once three-decker). Romald (Rumwald) was a Northumbrian prince who exhibited remarkably precocious signs of sanctity.

ROOS   ALL SAINTS   ER (H) TA 2830
Cobble and rubble building of many periods but largely Perp. EE arcade, two Dec. windows. Tower built c. 1442. Victorian porch (1842 restoration). Vestry (anchorage?) originally two-storeyed with attractive stair-turret and window from upper floor looking into church. Medieval, seventeenth- and eighteenth-century glass fragments in clerestory. Pulpit of 1615 and rood-screen of 1913+ (Temple Moore).

ROSSINGTON   ST MICHAEL   WR (SY) SK 6298
Largely of 1844 but there is a Norman doorway and chancel-arch and a Perp. tower. Norman font and rare medieval wooden pulpit. East window by Capronnier (1862).

ROTHERHAM   ALL SAINTS   WR (SY) SK 4492
One of most impressive parish churches of Yorkshire. Restored in eighteenth century and 1875 but substantially Perp. with magnificent

tower and spire. Good panelled nave ceiling with bosses. Fine stalls of 1452, contemporary benches and south chapel screen. Good pulpit of 1604 with tester added in eighteenth century. Organ case of same century. Norman font.

ROTHWELL   HOLY TRINITY   WR (WY) SE 3428
Large Perp. church, over-restored in 1873 (particularly affecting aisles and clerestory). Modest 1662 font with splendid contemporary cover. Nineteenth-century reredos and heraldic glass. Late A/S stones inset in south aisle walls. Faviell monument (1842).

ROUTH   ALL HALLOWS   ER (H) TA 0843
Largely restored in 1904 (when 'Perp.' tower was built). One EE and several Dec. windows. Defaced early fourteenth-century effigy. Good canopied brass of c. 1410.

ROWLEY   ST PETER   ER (H) SE 9732
Heavily restored Perp. exterior. Trans. south arcade, EE doorway and north arcade. South chapel added in 1730 to house memorials of Bradshaw family.

ROYSTON   ST JOHN BAPTIST   WR (SY) SE 3611
Big Perp. tower with heraldic decoration and unique oriel window. Church almost entirely Perp. with good original roofs. Perp. font with Jacobean cover. Perp. parclose screens. Faint traces of wall-painting. Notable monuments of 1673+ and 1754+.

RUDBY-IN-CLEVELAND: see HUTTON RUDBY

RUDSTON   ALL SAINTS   ER (H) TA 0967
Norman tower, EE arcades, Dec. chancel. Much later nineteenth-century restoration. Norman font, Dec. sedilia. Two large nineteenth-century memorials. Churchyard contains largest standing-stone in Britain. Prehistoric pagan monument converted into a 'rood-stone' by incised cross.

RYTHER   ALL SAINTS   WR (NY) SE 5539
Restoration in 1898 added pretty bell-turret but the chancel-arch may

be late A/S. Late Norman work in south doorway, EE west front, Dec. south aisle (with some contemporary glass fragments) and chancel. Five recovered altar-tables. South aisle has a splendid collection of Ryther monuments of fourteenth and fifteenth centuries.

SALTON ST JOHN OF BEVERLEY   NR (NY) SE 7180
Substantial church of two Norman builds. Tower-arch later thirteenth century (part of repairs after fire?). Fine medieval parish chest. 'Jacobean' pulpit of 1639. Nineteenth-century Dawker memorials. This title refers to an eighth-century Yorkshireman, monastic founder, teacher and bishop.

SANCTON ALL SAINTS   ER (H) SE 8939
Rebuilding of 1871 fortunately spared the fifteenth-century octagonal tower (unique in ER). The 'low side' lancet seems original EE, others are copies. Perp. font. Good ledger stones. Nearby A/S burial-ground to west of church testifies to large settlement (which, together with dedication, argues for original A/S church on site).

SANDAL MAGNA ST HELEN   WR (W) SE 3418
Largely Dec. cruciform church (chancel lengthened in nineteenth century) which was given aisles and a south chapel in Perp. period. There is Norman evidence in lower halves of crossing-piers. Perp. parclose screen, sixteenth-century bench ends, 1662 font, rare cast-iron 'ledgers', c. 1700. Fragments of medieval glass.

SAXTON ALL SAINTS   WR (NY) SE 4736
Norman origins with thirteenth-century modifications and Perp. tower. A/S cross-head possibly of tenth century. Seventeenth-century ledger stones. Elegant eighteenth-century monument to Hawke children. Churchyard has very rare external tomb-chest (Lord Dacre, killed at Towton battle in 1461).

SCALBY ST LAWRENCE   NR (NY) TA 0070
Trans. south arcade, EE chancel, tower of 1683, eighteenth-century windows in nave. Jacobean pulpit (with hourglass stand). Poor-box. Good monument of 1790.

St Patrick, Patrington, Humberside. (Derek G. Widdicombe (photo: Brian Jackson))

St Peter and St Leonard, Horbury, West Yorkshire. (Derek G. Widdicombe)

St Peter, Conisbrough, South Yorkshire

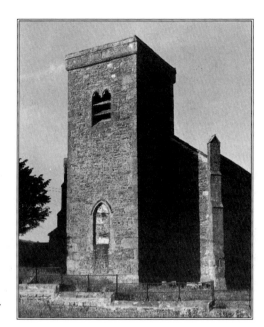

St Oswald, Castle Bolton,
Wensleydale, North Yorkshire.
(Derek G. Widdicombe)

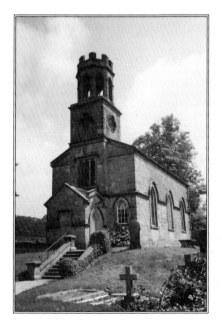

St Helen, Denton, West Yorkshire

All Saints, Brompton-by-Sawdon, near Scarborough, Yorkshire. (Derek G. Widdicombe)

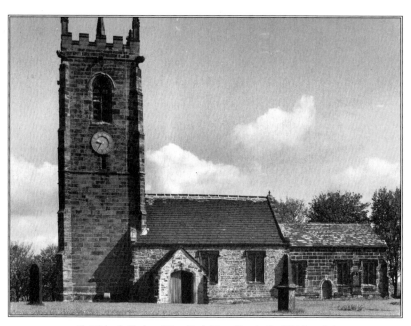

St Michael, Emley, West Yorkshire. (Derek G. Widdicombe)

St Andrew, Weaverthorpe, North Yorkshire. (Derek G. Widdicombe)

St Nicholas, Bradfield, South Yorkshire. (Derek G. Widdicombe)

St Mary, Gate Helmsley, North Yorkshire

SCARBOROUGH ST MARY   NR (NY) TA 0388

Trans. cruciform church lost chancel and two west towers in Civil
War. Weakened crossing-tower collapsed in 1659, rebuilt 1669. Much
Victorian remodelling. East window 1957. The outer aisles and two-
storeyed south porch date from *c.* 1350. (North outer aisle rebuilt
c. 1850.) Victorian chancel-screen of iron incorporates pulpit and
lectern. Remarkable collection of eighteenth-century brass plates
from headstones. Many monuments and tablets. Anne Bronte's grave
in churchyard.

ST MARTIN

Fine church of 1862 by Bodley with much pre-Raphaelite painting
(altar wall, ceiling, pulpit, glass, organ case). Reredos and rood-screen
by Bodley.

SCAWTON ST MARY   NR (NY) SE 5483

Small Norman church carefully restored in 1892. Low side window.
Twelfth-century sedilia reduced to one-seater, thirteenth-century
piscina. Opposite is mysterious recessed tank of twelfth century,
presumably serving as some kind of laver. (Above it is a Jacobean
aumbry.) Norman font with seventeenth-century cover.

SCRUTON ST RADEGUND   NR (NY) SE 2992

Considerable rebuilding in 1865 has left Perp. tower, Norman doorway
and buttress, EE arcades and lancets in chancel. High Victorian
furniture includes stone pulpit, reading-desk and lectern. East window
in same mood by Capronnier (1866). Radegund was a Frankish queen
who founded a nunnery at Poitiers where she died in 587.

SEAMER, SCARBOROUGH ST MARTIN   NR (NY) TA 0183

Considerable Norman church with tower heightened in thirteenth
century when clerestory was added (and modified later). Norman
doorway (perhaps contemporary ironwork on door) and sagging
chancel-arch. Perp. north chapel, north arcade, vestry and
battlements. Good Jacobean screen and pulpit panels. Fifteenth-
century glass fragments. Nineteenth-century monuments.

SEATON ROSS ST EDMUND   ER (H) SE 7741

Brick church of 1788, well restored in 1908, preserving eighteenth-century pulpit and communion rail. East window by Stammers (1953), described by Pevsner as 'wildly Expressionist'.

SEDBERGH ST ANDREW WR (C) SD 6592

Typical WR Perp. exterior with tower corbelled out in Leeds regional manner. But there is Norman work in north doorway, Trans. in arcades, and Dec. in south aisle and doorway. Restored 1886. Poor-box dated 1633. Pulpit with fine inlaid tester of eighteenth century. Good dripstones. Lych-gate. Dawson monument of 1820.

SELBY ST MARY AND ST GERMAIN WR (NY) SE 6132

Magnificent abbey church saved by townsfolk for continuing parochial use. Main building began in *c.* 1100 with chancel rebuilt *c.* 1300. Central tower fell in 1690, severely damaging south transept. Restorations in later nineteenth century. Whole fabric swept by fire in 1906. Main repairs completed by 1912. Upper stages added to west towers in 1935. Fine fifteenth-century font cover rescued from fire and much fourteenth-century glass restored in east window. Dec. sedilia. Communion rail of 1908. Fifteenth-century alabaster panel. Early fourteenth-century effigy and badly damaged one on tomb-chest of 1411+. Unique stone figures looking down from triforium.

Germain (Germanus) of Auxerre was a bishop who aided the British Church in early fifth century. The monk who founded Selby came from his abbey at Auxerre.

SETTRINGTON ALL SAINTS ER (NY) SE 8370

Built *c.* 1200 with added Perp. tower. Suffered several nineteenth-century restorations. Font and part of arcades survive from original building, also some fifteenth-century work. Chancel rebuilt 1867. Fragments of medieval glass in east window of south aisle. Brass of ejected Puritan minister. Masterman monument of 1769+.

SHERBURN ST HILDA ER (NY) SE 9576

Restored and extended in 1912. Tower and nave mainly late Norman with good chancel-arch. Part of chancel is Dec. Norman font and pillar piscina. Many fragments of A/S stone and medieval glass.

SHERBURN-IN-ELMET ALL SAINTS WR (NY) SE 4933

Mostly late Norman of which much survives: both arcades, west window, south doorway. Chancel rebuilt in EE period. Perp. windows, clerestory, tower top, north chapel. (Date of south chapel indeterminate, possibly seventeenth century). Magnificent fifteenth-century head of churchyard cross preserved in church. The churchyard has a Saxon cross on later shaft.

SHERIFF HUTTON   NR (NY) SE 6566

ST HELEN AND HOLY CROSS
Nave and tower originally Norman, latter raised in fifteenth century. Chancel rebuilt in thirteenth century, aisles had chapels added in fourteenth. Jacobean communion rail, a multitude of box pews (seventeenth to nineteenth centuries). Fourteenth-century glass fragments in north windows. Effigies include Richard III's son. Brass of 1491 with small engravings of children. Helen (of the title), mother of first Christian Roman emperor, is said to have discovered the actual cross on which Christ died.

SHIPTONTHORPE   ALL SAINTS   ER (H) SE 8543
Norman south door and contemporary statue in porch gable. Thirteenth-century tower and arcades. Dec. windows in north aisle and chancel. Restored 1883.

SIGGLESTHORNE   ST LAWRENCE   ER (H) TA 1545
Basically EE but much mended with brick (tower in 1676?). Chancel entirely built of brick. North arcade of 1827. Nineteenth-century monuments.

SILKSTONE   ALL SAINTS   WR (SY) SE 2805
Substantially Perp. apart from chancel, which was rebuilt in mid-nineteenth century. Fine exterior, exploiting detached pinnacles with tiny flying buttresses. Interior indicates previous church of c. 1200. South aisle terminates in sunken vestry (cf. Ecclesfield and Bradfield). Original Perp. roofs in nave and aisles with many bosses. Perp. screens. Seventeenth-century Wentworth monument. Royal Arms above tower-screen (carved both sides thus reversing supporters). Early nineteenth-century box pews. Memorial in churchyard to child-workers killed in 1838 colliery disaster.

SINNINGTON ALL SAINTS   NR (NY) SE 7485
Substantially restored in 1904 but quite a lot of Norman detail retained; for example, doorways (including crude tympanum of Sampson and lion (?)), window, piscina. Many A/S and A/D fragments inset in fabric. Seventeenth-century communion rail and benches.

SKEFFLING ST HELEN   ER (H) TA 3619
Perp. (1470) of cobble and rubble. Original chancel roof with bosses. Two family pews. Series of eighteenth-century tablets.

SKELBROOKE ST MICHAEL   WR (SY) SE 5012
Secluded church very much restored in 1872 after serious fire. Thirteenth-century tower. Canopied niche in north wall of nave. Local tradition claims Little John to be buried in churchyard. (Robin Hood's Well by side of old North Road is only a mile away.)

SKELTON, YORK ST GILES   NR (NY) SE 5656
Perfect small EE church of *c.* 1247 traditionally built by Minster masons. Continuous nave and chancel with bell-cote at their junction. Handsome piscina, twelfth-century statue bracket on east wall. Font of dubious date. Sparse furnishing.

SKERNE ST LEONARD   ER (H) TA 0455
Many Norman details in nave and chancel. North aisle of thirteenth century, as is low side window. Dec. east window and Perp. tower. Monuments of twelfth or thirteenth century displayed upright to bizarre effect.

SKIPSEA ALL SAINTS   ER (H) TA 1655
Cobbles laid in 'herring-bone' indicate eleventh-century date of nave and chancel. Perp. tower and south aisle. Arcades belong to mid-Victorian restoration. South door has early Norman ironwork. Circular churchyard is said to indicate former pagan holy site.

SKIPTON HOLY TRINITY   WR (NY) SD 9851
Mainly Perp. with some Dec. remnants and post-Civil War repairs. Porch of 1850. Good Perp. roofs. Dec. sedilia, fine Jacobean font cover to twelfth-century font, rood-screen of 1533 and parclose screens of Perp. period. Chancel dominated by Clifford tomb-chests.

Remains of anchorite's cell at west end of north aisle. Reredos of 1874.

SKIPWITH   ST HELEN   ER (NY) SE 6538
'One of noblest chancels in ER' (Pevsner) built about beginning of fourteenth century, but there is much older work. The lower part of the tower was originally the porch of an early A/S church, raised into a tower at beginning of eleventh century with doorway to wooden balcony facing east. A north aisle was added c. 1190 and south aisle shortly after. Some EE modifications to nave, and a late Perp. clerestory. Sculptured panel inside tower c. 1050, fine ironwork on south door (possibly thirteenth century), fragments of medieval glass, fifteenth-century screenwork (restored), almsbox dated 1615, sculpture of St Helen and St Simon Zelotes (1966).

SKIRLAUGH   ST AUGUSTINE   ER (H) TA 1537
A complete Perp. church given in 1401 to his native village by Walter Skirlaw, Bishop of Durham (1388–1406). A fine example of the latest style but loses its effect through the denuded interior. Only sparse fragments of medieval glass and mere traces of painting hint at former splendour.

SKIRPENBECK   ST MARY   ER (H) SE 7457
Norman nave, chancel and font. EE windows in chancel, meagre brick tower of eighteenth century. Paget monument (1636+).

SLAIDBURN   ST ANDREW   WR (L) SD 7152
Rebuilt in Perp. period including fine tower with unusual stair-turret. (There is one Dec. window in south chapel.) Magnificent contemporary roof. Eliz. font cover, good Jacobean chancel-screen, attractive eighteenth-century three-decker pulpit with box pews and family pews still preserving Georgian arrangement.

SNAITH   ST LAWRENCE   WR (H) SE 6422
Original Norman cruciform church largely obliterated by subsequent modifications: thirteenth-century tower and aisles, fourteenth-century chancel and later vestry, fifteenth-century arcades, chancel-arch and porch. Snaith was a priory cell of Selby Abbey whose last abbot was buried there (matrix only of magnificent brass memorial). Other

memorials include tomb-chest of *c.* 1500 and a monument by Chantrey.

SOUTH ANSTON ST JAMES WR (SY) SK 5183

Mostly Dec. (note especially east window, sedilia, double piscina in south aisle). The Perp. period added interesting tower and clerestory. Fine early fourteenth-century monument to lady and child. Much restored timber-framed porch. Curious churchyard 'ornament'.

SOUTH CAVE ALL SAINTS ER (H) SE 9130

EE and Dec. elements survive from reconstructions of 1601 and mid-nineteenth century. Perp. font (panels retooled), interesting monuments, good Charity Board (1809). East window may have eighteenth-century glass from Continent. Disused font is possibly Norman.

SOUTH COWTON ST MARY (R) NR (NY) NZ 2802

Entirely Perp. (1450–70), including tunnel-vaulted porch of two storeys (with 'Orate' inscription) and vestry with upper room. Remains of chancel-arch painting, medieval woodwork in stalls, screen and roof. Remains of three late fifteenth-century tomb-chests.

SOUTH KILVINGTON ST WILFRID NR (NY) SE 4283

Some Norman remains, including windows (others of late thirteenth century). Rebuilt chancel-arch may indicate former existence of stone screen. Perp. font with inscription. Fragments of medieval glass and some bench ends. Rare survival of hourglass. 'Gothic' stalls (near west end) carved by rector who was incumbent from 1859 to 1917 and died aged 101! Hat pegs on nave wall.

SOUTH KIRKBY ALL SAINTS WR (WY) SE 4410

Externally Perp. but thirteenth-century work in arcades and north chancel chapel. South chapel, tower and fine porch are Perp. Good aisle roofs with carved bosses and musicians. Tablet signed by Rysbrack.

SPEETON ST LEONARD ER (NY) TA 1574

Small, early Norman church standing alone on cliff-top. No east window. Twelfth-century relief of Agnus Dei inset in nave wall.

SPENNITHORNE   ST MICHAEL   NR (NY) SE 1489

Mostly Dec. exterior with good tower and elegant south aisle. North aisle is Perp. and north chapel *c.* 1620. EE arcades. Many small carvings on string-course, brackets, chancel-arch. Vaulted porch and tower (screen allegedly from Jervaulx). Faded eighteenth-century wall-painting. Simple sedilia. Chancel seat a construct of two medieval bench ends. Pre-Conquest sculpture built into exterior wall. Churchyard has Straubenzee family vault surmounted by looted cross from Crimea.

SPOFFORTH   ALL SAINTS   *WR (NY) SE 3650*

Apart from Perp. tower, exterior is of 1855 but there is a good deal of medieval work inside (mainly of late twelfth century). A/S cross-shaft fragment (*c.* 900). Badly preserved early fourteenth-century effigy in cusped recess. Churchyard has grave of 'Blind Jack of Knaresborough', the great civil engineer of late eighteenth century. Old rectory has medieval work.

SPROATLEY   ST SWITHIN   ER (H) TA 1934

Yellow brick walls of early nineteenth-century rebuilding with further remodelling in 1886, but worth visiting for unique thirteenth-century coffin lid with inscription in Norman French. Also more sentimental late nineteenth-century memorial to a child.

SPROTBOROUGH   ST MARY   WR (SY) SE 5302

Oldest parts are late thirteenth century (sedilia and piscina, for example). Dec. tower, heightened in Perp. period which also produced arcades, chancel-arch, fine nave ceiling and pretty niche in chancel. Pulpit is a construct of medieval panels with eighteenth-century tester. Interesting rood-screen of mid-fourteenth century with return stalls (three badly damaged misericords). Fine pewing of early and mid-sixteenth century. Jacobean communion rail. Interesting monuments of thirteenth, fourteenth and sixteenth centuries (including fine brass of 1474+). Mysterious stone seat ('Frith Stool') in chancel with fourteenth-century carving on what may be much older artefact.

STAINBURN   ST MARY (R)   WR (NY) SE 2448

Small, undeveloped Norman church now lying outside hamlet. Later windows (including seventeenth-century example with odd triangular head). Pulpit and pews of *c.* 1600. Good Norman font with Jacobean cover.

STAINTON   SS PETER AND PAUL   NR (Cl) SE 1097
Nave rebuilt *c.* 1800 and chancel in 1876 but chancel-arch is EE, tower and north transept Perp. The west doorway was renewed in eighteenth century. A/D fragments, fourteenth-century effigy, and eighteenth-century monuments.

STAINTON   ST WINIFRED   WR (SY) SK 5594
Norman chancel-arch, priest's doorway; late thirteenth-century windows; Dec. south chapel; Perp. tower. Fragments of fifteenth-century glass. Churchyard has good war memorial. Winifred was a seventh-century Welsh saint, killed at Holywell.

STANWICK   ST JOHN BAPTIST   NR (NY) SE 9871
Ruthless nineteenth-century restoration left some Norman masonry, EE tower, some windows and much of south aisle and porch. Many pre-Conquest sculptured fragments (including one of *c.* 800 inset in exterior of south wall). Many coffin lids in porch, four very worn effigies. Many later monuments (one with associated funeral armour).

STILLINGFLEET   ST HELEN   ER (NY) SE 5940
Magnificent south doorway and other Norman work. EE tower with Perp. top. Fine Dec. south chapel (founded 1336). Magnificent ironwork on south door with Viking characteristics. Jacobean parclose screens (some constructs). Early fourteenth-century effigy. Some late medieval glass and modern work by H.W. Harvey. Churchyard has grave of eleven choristers drowned in 1833 as they returned from carol-singing.

STILLINGTON   ST NICHOLAS   NR (NY) SE 5867
Originally Perp. but heavily restored in 1840. Some fragments of original glass in east window. Pleasant brick floor. Box pews. Royal Arms of 1739 (George II).

STOKESLEY   SS PETER AND PAUL   NR (NY) NZ 5208
Church, set in very attractive small town, has chancel (with remains of

sedilia) and tower of Perp. period but nave was completely rebuilt in 1771. There are two pleasant wall tablets of late eighteenth century.

STONEGRAVE   HOLY TRINITY   NR (NY) SE 6577

Norman tower with Perp. top but exterior entirely renewed in 1863. Internally, the north arcade is *c.* 1170 and the south a little later. Parts of the attractive chancel-screen of 1637 have been recycled to produce reredos, parclose screens and old panelling. Pulpit is roughly contemporary. Many interesting pre-Conquest fragments include fine tenth-century cross (standing on thirteenth-century coffin lid which surmounts A/D slab!). Early fourteenth-century effigy, unusually cross-legged for a civilian. Worn fifteenth-century effigies in canopied recess.

SUTTON   ST JAMES   ER (H) TA 1233

Still much a village church within Hull suburbia. Dec. stone chancel, brick tower and south side of *c.* 1400 remain of modifications made when church was made collegiate in 1347. EE font survives from earlier church. Monument to Sir John Sutton (†1357) who rebuilt chancel. Excellent Perp. screen (now between tower and north aisle). Painted panel from former pulpit.

SUTTON-ON-THE-FOREST   NR (NY) SE 5864

ALL HALLOWS

Apart from Perp. tower and south wall of nave, rebuilt in 1857 when rare timber north arcade was destroyed. East window is reused Dec. work and some south windows may be recycled Perp. Good eighteenth-century pulpit from which Laurence Sterne (vicar 1738–68) must have preached. Medieval glass fragments in west window. Some good eighteenth-century wall tablets.

SUTTON-UPON-DERWENT   ST MICHAEL   ER (H) SE 7046

Simple Norman church to which aisles were added in later twelfth century. The nave was extended and new aisle windows inserted in fourteenth century. More windows date from Perp. period when tower and porch were added. The east window is probably seventeenth century. Interesting late A/D cross-shaft and battered fourteenth-century representation of St George.

SWILLINGTON ST MARY WR (WY) SE 3830
Essentially Dec. with Perp. tower (rebuilt 1884), porch, doorway and clerestory. Fragments of oak effigy sealed in glass case. Arms of George I.

SWINE ST MARY ER (H) TA 1335
Generous parochial provision made c. 1180 by Cistercian nuns as extension to their simple (destroyed) church. Modifications in Dec. and Perp. periods and tower rebuilt in 1787 when font was possibly replaced. Pulpit dated 1619. Late medieval stalls with eight misericords. Good screens of 1531. Many Hilton monuments of fourteenth to fifteenth century, including a particularly fine one of c. 1400 in alabaster.

TADCASTER ST MARY WR (NY) SE 4843
As its site had become subject to regular flooding, the church was carefully dismantled and re-erected on a site 5 ft higher in 1875. A splendid Perp. building, embattled and much pinnacled, with remains of earlier work (Norman and Dec.). Fragments of medieval glass and fine east window by Morris (c. 1875). Early twentieth-century furniture.

TANKERSLEY ST PETER WR (SY) SK 3499
Dec. nave and chancel with porch unusually placed between them (good nineteenth-century gate). Perp. tower and clerestory. Aisle rebuilt in 1881. Morris glass in a south window, another by C. Webb. Many incised grave-slabs include one dated 1435.

TERRINGTON ALL SAINTS NR (NY) SE 6670
Perp. exterior but interior shows work from Norman period (window, north arcade, herring-bone masonry) and from fourteenth century (south chapel, chancel-arch). Good monument of 1816+.

THIRSK ST MARY NR (NY) SE 4282
Most spectacular Perp. church in NR (built c. 1450). Two-storeyed porch, crypt, very fine roof, contemporary traceried doors, parclose screens, bench ends, font cover, sedilia and fragments of glass. Seated Virgin above west window. Small Thirsk brass (1419+). Faded seventeenth-century murals of apostles on clerestory walls.

THORMANBY   ST MARY   NR (NY) SE 4974
Much altered Norman church whose brick tower was added in 1822.
The pleasant interior has good furnishings which include early
nineteenth-century pulpit with tester. The east window is *c*. 1900 by
Kempe and includes his 'logo' (wheat sheaf) which he began to use
about that time.

THORNE   ST NICHOLAS   WR (SY) SE 6813
Largely built round the turn of thirteenth and fourteenth centuries
with Perp. modifications which included heightened tower, chapels,
clerestory and two-storeyed porch (unusually provided with oriel
window). A number of early twentieth-century stained glass windows.

THORNER   ST PETER   WR (WY) SE 3740
Its Perp. tower (with top characteristic of area) dominates pleasant
village but, apart from west end, church largely dates from 1855.
Chancel has memorial to a man who lived from 1625 to 1742!

THORNGUMBALD   ST MARY   ER (H) TA 2026
Small, undeveloped church of *c*. 1200 with doorways of period
(priest's door re-set). Trans. font.

THORNHILL   ST MICHAEL   WR (WY) SE 2418
Oldest part is base of tower (thirteenth century) which was
heightened in Perp. period when chancel was remodelled and
provided with chapels. Nave rebuilt in 1777 and again in Victorian
period. Many interesting A/S fragments of *c*. 850 but treasure is Savile
Chapel (1447) with original roof, much glass and remarkable series of
monuments dating from fourteenth to twentieth centuries.

THORNTON   ST MICHAEL   ER (H) SE 7545
Largely of fourteenth to fifteenth century with some restoration and
rebuilding (west end) in 1892. Interesting medieval tracery and pretty
inlaid organ case of early nineteenth century.

THORNTON DALE   ALL SAINTS   NR (NY) SE 8382
Set in delightful village, church is Dec. (apart from chancel, rebuilt
1866). Fine early fourteenth-century monument to lady and one of
1773+ by Fisher of York.

THORNTON-IN-CRAVEN   ST MARY   WR (NY) SE 1233
Perp. church with low tower, somewhat outside village. Some simple
Perp. screenwork, seventeenth-century pews with traceried panels,
east window glass by Kempe (1898).

THORNTON-LE-STREET   ST LEONARD   NR (NY) SE 4186
Late Norman nave, rest largely fourteenth century and Victorian
(including bell-turret). Late seventeenth-century memorials and
Fisher monument (1792+). East window by Kempe (1894).

THORNTON STEWARD   ST OSWALD   NR (NY) SE 1787
Distant from present village, church retains A/S and Norman work.
Some pre-Conquest sculptured fragments. EE font, simple single-
seater sedile. Impressive early fourteenth-century tomb recess.

THORNTON WATLASS   ST MARY   NR (NY) SE 2385
Fine Dec. tower, rest of 1868 in Victorian Gothic. Lectern is a
construct, utilizing alleged ship's figure-head.

THORPE BASSET   ALL SAINTS   ER (NY) SE 8573
Almost completely rebuilt in 1880 but there is a Norman doorway, a
thirteenth-century north arcade and some fragments of medieval glass.
Decayed fourteenth-century effigy and finely sculptured small
thirteenth-century detached corbel.

THORPE SALVIN   ST PETER   WR (SY) SK 5281
Essentially Norman with chancel replaced in Dec. period (low side
window, pretty sedilia). Perp. tower top, some windows and
clerestory. Remarkable Norman font is one of most interesting in
country. Monuments of fifteenth, sixteenth and seventeenth centuries.
Half-timbered porch is a rare Yorkshire phenomenon.

THROAPHAM   ST JOHN   WR (SY) SK 5387
Norman doorway, EE arcades and chancel-arch. Perp. clerestory, windows
and north chapel; also font and screen under tower. Much worn but fine
late thirteenth-century coffin lid. Early seventeenth-century brass.

THRYBERGH   ST LEONARD   WR (SY) SK 4694
Generally Perp. in appearance but contains Norman work in nave,

while chancel is Dec. Remarkable number of monuments with examples from fourteenth and sixteenth to nineteenth centuries. Medieval glass in south aisle. Remains of medieval churchyard crosses in cemetery.

THWING   ALL SAINTS   ER (H) TA 0570

Generally late Victorian but Norman doorway (with tympanum) and chancel-arch survive, as does the font (though it was found at Sewerby). The north arcade was built in Perp. period when it was provided with a remarkable squint that involved the construction of a special external bulge for its accommodation. Fine fourteenth-century effigy of priest. Some Georgian heraldic glass. Many tablets.

TICKHILL   ST MARY   WR (SY) SK 5892

Proudest village church in WR and essentially Perp. (though it was largely a remodelling of thirteenth-century predecessor). Light and spacious interior retains parclose screen, glass in upper parts of south aisle windows and early sixteenth-century tomb-chest rescued when Austin friars' house was dissolved. Pulpit is a construct of traceried panels which are also reused elsewhere. Font may be nineteenth century rather than original Perp. (modern cover by G.G. Pace). Magnificent tower retains statuary and church is provided with both north and south porches.

TODWICK   SS PETER AND PAUL   WR (SY) SK 4984

Mainly Dec. but there are remains of Norman doorways, and chancel-arch is probably remodelled Norman work. Perp. tower. Seventeenth-century box pews and communion rail. Small brass of 1609.

TONG, BRADFORD   ST JAMES   WR (WY) SE 2130

Built 1727 close to his house by the owner of Tong Hall. Reuses some pieces of medieval church but basically classical and retains almost all its eighteenth-century furniture: three-decker pulpit, family pews for squire (with fireplace) and parson, box pews for rest, west gallery, communion rail.

TOPCLIFFE   ST COLUMBA   NR (NY) SE 3976

Built 1855 in Dec. style but used pieces from medieval church: east windows, sedilia and piscina. It also preserved one of best brasses in England (Thomas de Topcliffe and wife, 1391+). Other interesting features include Robinson monument (1688+) and window glass in south side of chancel which is an early effort (1857) by Burne-Jones. Columba was the sixth-century monk who founded the Abbey of Iona and played a major part in the conversion of Scotland. Unusual title in England.

TREETON   ST HELEN   WR (SY) SK 4387
Essentially Trans. but with features of thirteenth century and a Dec. chancel. Tower raised and clerestory added in Perp. period. Perp. woodwork in south chapel screen and some benches. Mutilated thirteenth-century effigy.

TUNSTALL   ALL SAINTS   ER (H) TA 3032
Largely built of cobble-stones. Norman work in chancel, EE doorway and window, Dec. tower, Perp. clerestory and windows. Font of *c.* 1300 with Perp. bowl (later recut).

UGGLEBARNBY   ALL SAINTS   NR (NY) NZ 8707
Built 1872 in EE style (some detached fragments from medieval church). Elaborate and rich High Victorian furnishings include hammer-beam roof, font and cover, reredos, pulpit and benches.

UPLEATHAM   ST ANDREW   NR (Cl) NZ 6319
Built 1835 in neo-Norman style but font is original. Old church, in fine setting about half a mile away, is one of many claimants to title of 'smallest church in England'. It consists of part of nave of Norman church with diminutive tower added in seventeenth century. Architectural fragments include part of Norman capital and A/D cross-head.

UPPER POPPLETON   ALL SAINTS   WR (NY) SE 5554
Built 1891 reusing Norman doorway and a Perp. window from medieval church. Lectern recycles some late fifteenth-century panels. Large eighteenth-century Flemish painting acquired in 1946.

WADWORTH   ST JOHN BAPTIST   WR (SY) SK 5697
Large Norman and Trans. church with building continuing into

thirteenth century. Chancel remodelled and north chapel added
c. 1300. South chapel is Dec. and slender tower Perp. (also some
windows and clerestory). Furnishings include medieval parish chest
and some very interesting fourteenth- and fifteenth-century
monuments.

WAKEFIELD   ALL SAINTS   WR (WY) SE 3320

In spite of being raised to Anglican cathedral status in 1888, it has
largely remained a town parish church. Perp. exterior with highest
spire in Yorkshire. The church developed from *c.* 1150 to take up its
present form in fifteenth century. Font of 1661, good chancel-screen
of 1635 (with rood of 1950). Late fifteenth-century quire stalls (some
with misericords), one medieval bench end, eighteenth-century
pulpit, organ case and gate to south porch, much Kempe glass. Plaster
cast of A/S cross-shaft removed to York Museum.

WALES   ST JOHN BAPTIST   WR (SY) SK 4782

Original Norman church made into north aisle of much larger
church in 1897. Norman font and some Perp. work (including roof)
survive. Some medieval glass panels brought in from Continent.

WALKINGTON   ALL HALLOWS   ER (H) SE 9936

Largely rebuilt (in brick) in 1818 but there is work of *c.* 1200
(arches and south doorway), one Dec. and many Perp. windows.
Perp. tower probably seventeenth century, as is pulpit. Slab engraved
with chalice.

WALTON   ST PETER   WR (WY) SK 4447

Norman tower with Perp. top. Rest mainly *c.* 1340–50. Low side
window. Elaborate fourteenth-century recess contains badly preserved
effigy. Jacobean pulpit, with panels added in nineteenth century.

WATH   ST MARY   NR (NY) SE 3277

Pleasantly sited. Norman church known from excavation to have
once possessed an apse. Present chancel of *c.* 1300. Perp. windows and
vestry (originally two-storeyed). Tower built in 1812. South chapel
with tomb recess of *c.* 1330. Many A/S fragments. Splendid
fourteenth-century parish chest. Fragment of medieval glass. Many
monuments include two fifteenth-century brasses.

WATH-UPON-DEARNE ALL SAINTS   WR (SY) SE 4300
Norman work includes lower tower, north arcade and north chapel.
There is thirteenth-century work in chancel, north transept, etc.
Porch of *c.* 1300. Perp. tower top and clerestory, bench ends and
chest. Bell dated 1588 under tower. Early nineteenth-century brass
chandeliers.

WATTON ST MARY   ER (H) TA 0150
Brick church probably rebuilt in Perp. period but possibly *c.* 1600.
There are reused EE windows and possibly Perp. ones. Severe
external outline and (uncompleted) open timber roof. Seventeenth-
century communion rail. Early (*c.* 1260) incised slab to William de
Malton, prior of neighbouring Gilbertine house.

WAWNE ST PETER   ER (H) TA 0836
Largely EE apart from Perp. tower top, clerestory, battlements, south
doorway and some windows. Good nave roof with bosses, finely
austere EE sedilia and piscina, Perp. font.

WEAVERTHORPE ST ANDREW   ER (NY) SE 9670
Fine Norman church with impressive slim tower. Norman font, some
windows of *c.* 1300. Good nave roof of 1872 by Street who also
produced metal screen and pulpit. Reredos and statue of St Andrew
are nineteenth century as is glass by Clayton and Bell. South doorway
has sundial with record of Norman building. Fourteenth-century
effigy (much decayed) in churchyard.

WELL ST MICHAEL   NR (NY) SE 2682
Late Norman doorway, some EE work apparently modified in Dec.
period when south aisle was added and other modifications made. Perp.
some windows, clerestory and tower. South chapel arcade is a Victorian
restoration. Rare Dec. font cover. Reredos in north chapel is sixteenth-
century Dutch. Fourteenth-century glass in east window of south aisle
(with Victorian supplements). Sixteenth-century and later monuments.
Roman mosaic from nearby villa attached to west wall of nave.
Remarkably high shaft remains of former churchyard cross.

WELTON ST HELEN   ER (H) SE 9527
Practically rebuilt in 1863 but pieces of medieval work survive,

including a pleasant Perp. piscina and a defaced early fourteenth-century effigy. Six Morris windows which may be compared with slightly earlier glass by Capronnier in south window of south transept.

WELWICK   ST MARY   ER (H) TA 3421
Some EE work but lavishly modified in Dec. period. Badly mauled remains of fine tomb of *c.* 1360. Perp. clerestory and screen. Brass of 1621 commemorating elder brother of two men involved in 'Gunpowder Plot'. Early eighteenth-century pulpit with tester.

WENSLEY   HOLY TRINITY   NR (NY) SE 0989
Mid-thirteenth-century chancel with sedilia and piscina. More building *c.* 1300 produced arcades, chancel-arch, aisle windows. Perp. two-storeyed sacristy with barred upper window. Remarkably interesting furniture includes A/S fragments, remains of fourteenth-century murals, an alleged wooden reliquary, fragments of medieval glass, Scrope pew (seventeenth century recycling early sixteenth-century screen), seating from seventeenth and eighteenth centuries, two-decker pulpit, font and cover (1662), late seventeenth-century communion rail, Wenslaw brass (late fourteenth-century) Scrope memorial (1525+).

WEST HESLERTON   ALL SAINTS   ER (NY) SE 9175
EE chancel with fine later Easter Sepulchre, rest mainly Victorian restoration. Font dated 1853. East window by Kempe (1893). Sykes monument (1805+) with extended eulogy.

WESTON   ALL SAINTS   WR (NY) SE 1747
Close neighbour to 'big house'. Attractive west front displays Norman, fifteenth-, sixteenth- and seventeenth-century work. Main building in Norman period, enlarged in fifteenth century and restored in 1819. Interior has box pews around big three-decker pulpit and 'squire's parlour' with fireplace. Some eighteenth-century heraldic glass. Vavasour monuments.

WESTOW   ST MARY   ER (NY) SE 7565
Somewhat isolated. Almost entirely rebuilt in 1864 but retains original Perp. tower and some medieval masonry. Norman font and panel of crucifixion which, curiously, is obverse of cresset-stone (now

invisible due to incorporation in memorial). A/S cross-head. East window by Wailes (1864).

WEST ROUNTON   ST OSWALD   NR (NY) NZ 4103
A Norman church but, apart from south doorway and chancel-arch, 'Neo-Norman' of 1860. A real Norman font with incomprehensible iconography. Stained glass by H. Stammers.

WEST TANFIELD   ST NICHOLAS   NR (NY) SE 2778
Norman doorway, EE arcade, rest Perp. (apart from Victorian restoration of 1860). Mysterious recess in north chapel which may have been miniature chantry. A/S sculptured fragment, some substantial bits of fifteenth-century glass and many monuments (one retaining its hearse) of Marmion family whose castle gatehouse neighbours the church. Also brass commemorating rector who died c. 1492.

WETWANG   ST NICHOLAS   ER (H) SE 9359
A Norman church, modified in thirteenth century when, among other things, tower was added (made higher c. 1400). Transepts (one lost) were added in late thirteenth century and there was a restoration in 1902. Norman font, and fragments in south wall of tower. Good modern furnishings.

WHARRAM-LE-STREET   ST MARY   ER (NY) SE 8666
A/S masonry in nave and lower tower (heightened c. 1100 when other Norman modifications took place). Fourteenth-century north aisle (which contains eighteenth-century communion table). Chancel rebuilt in 1864.

WHENBY   ST MARTIN (R)   NR (NY) SE 6370
Thirteenth-century church almost completely rebuilt in Perp. period (restorations in 1871 and 1910). Heavily battlemented except on north side. Remains of fifteenth-century chancel-screen with traces of colouring. Many medieval benches in nave. Seventeenth-century screen to north chapel retains original latch and hinges. Curious blocked door in east wall of chancel.

WHISTON   ST MARY MAGDALENE   WR (SY) SK 4490
Largely rebuilt in 1883 but retains Norman tower and some masonry

(in old nave, now aisle of much enlarged church). Three windows by Kempe (1883–91).

WHITBY ST MARY   NR (NY) NZ 8911

Medieval work is mostly Norman and EE but much obscured by heavy and insensitive Georgian modifications. The interior is a unique survival of post-Reformation arrangements before late nineteenth-century reaction, presenting a conglomeration of pews, galleries, staircases, and domestic-type windows with focus divided between Cholmley pew and three-decker pulpit. Two disused Perp. fonts (brought in), great chandelier of 1769. Good gravestones in churchyard.

WHITGIFT ST MARY MAGDALENE   WR (H) SE 8022

Largely dates from early fourteenth century but much Perp. modification (including tower whose upper stages have internal brick facing) and later restoration. Seventeenth-century or earlier benches. Curious clock face.

WHITKIRK ST MARY   WR (WY) SE 3634

Sturdy village church in what is practically a suburb of Leeds. Perp. apart from chancel rebuilt in 1901. Scargill monument of *c.* 1550 and eighteenth-century Irwin memorial. Eighteenth-century tablet to engineer John Smeeton.

WHIXLEY ASCENSION   WR (NY) SE 4457

Unique (possibly altered) dedication of church whose Norman origin is testified by one window. Rest (apart from Perp. tower) is essentially Dec. and provides a rare example of a village church in one predominant style. Tancred monument (1754+).

WHORLTON-IN-CLEVELAND   NR (NY) NZ 4802

HOLY CROSS

Old church: remotely situated at end of yew avenue. Norman church with Perp. tower in ruinous condition. Dec. chancel largely intact and contains remarkably fine oak effigy of early fourteenth century. Large new church built 1877 has some Kempe glass.

WIGHILL   ALL SAINTS   WR (NY) SE 4746

Very fine Norman doorway with unusual capital carvings (well preserved). Norman north arcade and interesting furnishings which include Jacobean pulpit, communion rail, and low chancel-screen. Pews with crude poppy-heads may be earlier. Some fifteenth-century glass fragments. Good Stapleton monuments.

WILBERFOSS   ST JOHN BAPTIST   ER (H) SE 7350

Perp. with tower and south aisle. Once attached to Benedictine nunnery of which nothing survives. Small brass to Robert Hoton and wife (1447+).

WILLERBY, NR FILEY   ST PETER   ER (NY) TA 0179

Thirteenth century (including later tower). South door preserves hinges from the same century.

WILTON   ST CUTHBERT   NR (Cl) NZ 5819

In grounds of grand early nineteenth-century castle. Norman, but much hacked about in 1908 and west front could be contemporary with castle. Thirteenth-century low side window, some Norman fragments and badly preserved but interesting early fourteenth-century effigies in porch.

WINESTEAD   ST GERMAN   ER (H) TA 2924

Largely rebuilt in Perp. period (Norman fragment in chancel south wall), further restoration c. 1900. Good Perp. quire-screen, brass inscription to rector (1418+), early sixteenth-century brass, fragment of fifteenth-century glass. Medieval and Hildyard monuments (especially in Jacobean family chapel with contemporary screen). Late seventeenth-century pulpit.

WINTRINGHAM   ST PETER   ER (NY) SE 8873

Norman chancel and font, rest Dec. and Perp. with particularly fine Perp. tower. Nave roof and poor-box of late seventeenth century. Font cover of 1736 with painted cherubs. Tower-screen dated 1723, Perp. parclose screens, handsome Jacobean pews. Both pulpit and reader's desk reuse Jacobean panels. Unusually substantial survival of fourteenth-century glass in south aisle. Interesting memorial of 1651.

WISTOW   ALL SAINTS   WR (NY) SE 5835

There is EE and Dec. work but the impression is predominantly Perp. Fragments of medieval glass in west window of north aisle, interesting coffin lid with Lombardic lettering (*c.* 1200), fine gabled recess in chancel (*c.* 1320), Jacobean pulpit.

WOMERSLEY   ST MARTIN   WR (NY) SE 5319

Cruciform church with good broach spire. Scant Norman remains, more EE, but Dec. is dominant (tower, spire, south arcade and most windows, for example). No east window. Much brought in furniture includes fine Flemish sculpture, Baroque Italian candlesticks and representation of last supper in seventeenth-century Spanish tilework. Roofs and complete rood-screen by Bodley, *c.* 1895. Early fourteenth-century effigy. Kempe glass.

WOODKIRK   ST MARY   WR (WY) SE 2625

Rebuilt *c.* 1830 but EE tower survives as well as good fifteenth-century stalls in chancel and Jacobean pulpit.

WOOLLEY   ST PETER   WR (WY) SE 3113

Entirely Perp. though there is a Norman tympanum re-set in south aisle. Perp. bench ends, chapel screen and glass fragments. West window of south aisle has good glass of 1871, probably from Morris workshops.

WORSBOROUGH   ST MARY   WR (SY) SE 3402

Norman work in chancel with Dec. east window. Tower is also Dec. with top added in Perp. period when there was a good deal of remodelling (arcades, chancel chapels, vestry, porch with good roof). Fine Perp. south door with inscription. Restoration of 1838 increased height and produced many windows. Eighteenth-century Squire's Pew. Interesting monuments, especially rare two-tier erection in timber (1534+).

WRAGBY   ST MICHAEL   WR (WY) SE 4017

Large, entirely Perp. church in grounds of big house (Nostell Priory). Chancel rebuilt by prior in 1533 (east window has pieces of contemporary glass). Norman font retained from original church. Georgian organ case, eighteenth-century pulpit ('brought in' from Germany or Italy, as was remarkable collection of sixteenth- to eighteenth-century stained glass). Winn monuments.

WYCLIFFE   ST MARY   NR (D) NZ 1114

Apart from Victorian east window, architecture is largely EE. Later Dec. windows (with some contemporary glass). Interesting monuments include good hog-back, incised slab (1456+) and brass of 1606+. Eighteenth-century chandeliers, bishop's chair, good modern ceilings, woodwork by Thompson of Kilburn.

YARM   ST MARY MAGDALENE   NR (Cl) NZ 4112

By river, away from present town centre. Rebuilt in 1730 but retains curious Norman west front with medieval modifications. Interior remodelled in Victorian period. Perp. font with Jacobean cover (knob added in eighteenth century). A/S fragments, recycled fourteenth-century effigies. Peckitt glass (1768) in south window.

YORK   (NY) SE 6052

Medieval York had some thirty parish churches of which nineteen survive in varying states and usage.

ALL SAINTS, NORTH ST.

Perhaps the most rewarding. Roman masonry in its Norman core but mostly of fifteenth century. The restoration in early twentieth century replaced rood-screen and added curious anchorage outside west end. Its treasure is the outstanding amount of medieval stained glass (mainly early fifteenth century) which includes the famous 'Pricke of Conscience' and 'Corporal Works of Mercy'. Fine roofs with repainted bosses and corbels. Stalls (one misericord) of later fifteenth century.

ALL SAINTS, PAVEMENT

Much knocked about: chancel demolished in eighteenth century, and over-restored in nineteenth, but preserves fine tower of *c.* 1500 and some interesting furniture. Fragment of Saxon tombstone, thirteenth-century door-knocker, fifteenth-century lectern (much altered), pulpit with tester (1634), seventeenth-century brass and, above all, west window of late fourteenth-century glass.

HOLY TRINITY, GOODRAMGATE (R)

Largely Perp. building set back from street with unrestored interior whose largely eighteenth-century furnishings rise from an undulating floor. Fourteenth- and fifteenth-century glass, especially in east window (1470).

HOLY TRINITY, MICKLEGATE

Thirteenth-century work surviving from truncated remains of former priory church. Much 'restored' in nineteenth century with better work of *c.* 1902. Perp. tower. Architectural fragments, font cover (1717), organ case (1964 by G.G. Pace), Kempe glass (1904–7). Fifteenth-century door with tracery. Stocks in churchyard.

ST CUTHBERT, PEASEHOLME GREEN

Reputedly York's oldest parish church (Saxon origin and reusing Roman masonry). Rebuilt in Perp. period (from whence much of roof timber survives). Crypt. Jacobean pulpit. Heraldic glass. Early nineteenth-century cast-iron font.

ST DENYS, WALMGATE

Original cruciform church lost in modification and demolition (nave destroyed 1798, tower rebuilt 1847). Reset Norman doorway, fine fourteenth-century east window, fifteenth-century nave roof (former chancel), Jacobean pulpit, some excellent glass of fourteenth to fifteenth century.

ST HELEN, ST HELEN'S SQUARE

Thirteenth century, but largely rebuilt in reign of Queen Mary (1550s). Victorian restoration included rebuilding tower. EE font. Fine small sculptures on corbels of south arcade (Dec.). Disappointing glass in what was guild church of York glaziers.

ST MARTIN-CUM-GREGORY, MICKLEGATE

Trans. and Perp. church now used as youth centre. Jacobean pulpit, much fine eighteenth-century furniture, medieval glass and work by Peckitt (who is buried here).

ST MARTIN-LE-GRAND, CONEY ST.

Severely damaged in the Second World War but ingeniously reconstituted by G.G. Pace (1961 ff.). Impressive replaced fifteenth-century window depicting life of St Martin, many medieval fragments, east window by H. Stammers and contemporary reredos by F. Roper.

Brass (1614+), font cover (1717), organ case by Pace. Fine clock (originally 1688, restored 1966) on bracket overhanging street.

ST MARY BISHOPHILL JUNIOR

Tower is oldest ecclesiastical building in York, representing three phases of A/S architecture and in bottom stage reuses Roman material. Church largely nineteenth century but retains Trans. and Dec. work. Modern bosses on medieval roof, A/S stone and medieval glass fragments, seventeenth-century font cover, reredos of *c.* 1900 (T. Moore).

ST MARY, CASTLEGATE

Some pre-Conquest masonry and rare dedication stone of *c.* 1020. Present building essentially Perp. and restoration of 1870. Fine tower with lantern and highest spire in York. Interior largely gutted to accommodate 'Heritage Centre'.

ST MICHAEL-LE-BELFREY, PETERGATE

Norman origins but completely rebuilt in 1525–*c.* 1536 (remodelled in later nineteenth century). Eighteenth-century furnishings include gallery (with Royal Arms), reredos and communion rail. Original Perp. benches and Victorian box pews. Fourteenth-century glass in east window and good early sixteenth-century work elsewhere. Eighteenth-century tablets and monuments. Guy Fawkes was baptized here.

ST MICHAEL, SPURRIERGATE

Church and tower reduced and much rebuilt in nineteenth century but restoration of 1965+ (G.G. Pace) has produced fine interior. Trans. and Perp. building and good eighteenth-century furnishings (communion table, reredos and rail), late seventeenth-century frontal in stamped leather and remarkable door surround of *c.* 1700. Much excellent fifteenth-century glass.

ST OLAVE, MARYGATE

No remains of known A/D church which was eventually rebuilt in Perp. style. Much damaged in Civil War (upper tower and arcades rebuilt in 1772). More complete rebuilding around 1900. Font of 1673 with 1963 cover by G.G. Pace. Medieval glass in middle of east window. Twentieth-century copper crucifix over pulpit. York artist William Etty is buried in churchyard.